Whiteness and Nationalism

Naming whiteness is an increasingly pressing issue across a variety of social and political contexts. In this book, an international set of authors discuss how and why this has come to be the case.

Studying whiteness, as either a social identity or political ideology, is a relatively recent area of scholarship. Unusually, within the fields of race and ethnicity, it is a concept that sits at an intersection between historical privilege and identity. At the same time, 'white privilege' is not universally shared in (or can be distant to) how many white people feel they experience their identities. Whiteness as a site of privilege is therefore not absolute, but rather cross-cut by a range of other concerns, too. Nonetheless, recent political developments serve to illustrate the political potency of appeals to whiteness, in a way that suggests whiteness coupled with nationhood is a central social and political topic.

In this book, authors from the USA, Australia and Europe consider the contemporary relationships between whiteness and national identity by focusing on mainstream electoral politics, the 'normalisation' of white supremacy and where whiteness stands in relation to pluralised national identities.

The chapters in this book were originally published as a special issue of the journal *Identities: Global Studies in Culture and Power*.

Nasar Meer is Professor of Race, Identity and Citizenship and Director of RACE.ED at the University of Edinburgh, UK. He is a Royal Society of Edinburgh Research Fellow and Principal Investigator of the H2020-funded project Governance and Local Integration of Migrants and Europe's Refugees (GLIMER). He is a recipient of the Thomas Reid Medal for Excellence in the Social Sciences and former Minda de Gunzberg Fellow at Harvard University, USA.

Whiteness and Nationalism

Edited by
Nasar Meer

LONDON AND NEW YORK

First published 2021
by Routledge
2 Park Square, Milton Park, Abingdon, Oxon OX14 4RN

and by Routledge
52 Vanderbilt Avenue, New York, NY 10017

Routledge is an imprint of the Taylor & Francis Group, an informa business

© 2021 Taylor & Francis

All rights reserved. No part of this book may be reprinted or reproduced or utilised in any form or by any electronic, mechanical, or other means, now known or hereafter invented, including photocopying and recording, or in any information storage or retrieval system, without permission in writing from the publishers.

Trademark notice: Product or corporate names may be trademarks or registered trademarks, and are used only for identification and explanation without intent to infringe.

British Library Cataloguing in Publication Data
A catalogue record for this book is available from the British Library

ISBN 13: 978-0-367-89541-9

Typeset in Myriad Pro
by Newgen Publishing UK

Publisher's Note
The publisher accepts responsibility for any inconsistencies that may have arisen during the conversion of this book from journal articles to book chapters, namely the inclusion of journal terminology.

Disclaimer
Every effort has been made to contact copyright holders for their permission to reprint material in this book. The publishers would be grateful to hear from any copyright holder who is not here acknowledged and will undertake to rectify any errors or omissions in future editions of this book.

Contents

Citation Information	vi
Notes on Contributors	viii
Introduction: The wreckage of white supremacy *Nasar Meer*	1
1 Whiteness, populism and the racialisation of the working class in the United Kingdom and the United States *Aurelien Mondon and Aaron Winter*	10
2 Denmark's blond vision and the fractal logics of a nation in danger *Peter Hervik*	29
3 Are French people white?: Towards an understanding of whiteness in Republican France *Jean Beaman*	46
4 The whiteness of cultural boundaries in France *Angéline Escafré-Dublet*	63
5 Reimagining racism: understanding the whiteness and nationhood strategies of British-born South Africans *Pauline Leonard*	79
6 Securing whiteness?: Critical Race Theory (CRT) and the securitization of Muslims in education *Damian Breen and Nasar Meer*	95
7 Looking as white: anti-racism apps, appearance and racialized embodiment *Alana Lentin*	114
Index	131

Citation Information

The chapters in this book were originally published in *Identities: Global Studies in Culture and Power*, volume 26, issue 5 (October 2019). When citing this material, please use the original page numbering for each article, as follows:

Introduction
The wreckage of white supremacy
Nasar Meer
Identities: Global Studies in Culture and Power, volume 26, issue 5 (October 2019), pp. 501–509

Chapter 1
Whiteness, populism and the racialisation of the working class in the United Kingdom and the United States
Aurelien Mondon and Aaron Winter
Identities: Global Studies in Culture and Power, volume 26, issue 5 (October 2019), pp. 510–528

Chapter 2
Denmark's blond vision and the fractal logics of a nation in danger
Peter Hervik
Identities: Global Studies in Culture and Power, volume 26, issue 5 (October 2019), pp. 529–545

Chapter 3
Are French people white?: Towards an understanding of whiteness in Republican France
Jean Beaman
Identities: Global Studies in Culture and Power, volume 26, issue 5 (October 2019), pp. 546–562

Chapter 4
The whiteness of cultural boundaries in France
Angéline Escafré-Dublet
Identities: Global Studies in Culture and Power, volume 26, issue 5 (October 2019), pp. 563–578

Chapter 5
Reimagining racism: understanding the whiteness and nationhood strategies of British-born South Africans
Pauline Leonard
Identities: Global Studies in Culture and Power, volume 26, issue 5 (October 2019), pp. 579–594

Chapter 6
Securing whiteness?: Critical Race Theory (CRT) and the securitization of Muslims in education
Damian Breen and Nasar Meer
Identities: Global Studies in Culture and Power, volume 26, issue 5 (October 2019), pp. 595–613

Chapter 7
Looking as white: anti-racism apps, appearance and racialized embodiment
Alana Lentin
Identities: Global Studies in Culture and Power, volume 26, issue 5 (October 2019), pp. 614–630

For any permission-related enquiries please visit:
www.tandfonline.com/page/help/permissions

Notes on Contributors

Jean Beaman, Department of Sociology, University of California, Santa Barbara, CA, USA.

Damian Breen, School of Social Sciences, Birmingham City University, UK.

Angéline Escafré-Dublet, Department of Political Science, Université Lumière Lyon 2, France.

Peter Hervik, Institute for Culture and Global Studies, University of Aalborg, Denmark.

Alana Lentin, School of Humanities and Communication Arts, Western Sydney University, Australia.

Pauline Leonard, School of Economic, Political and Social Sciences, University of Southampton, UK.

Nasar Meer, School of Social and Political Sciences, The University of Edinburgh, UK.

Aurelien Mondon, Department of Politics, Languages and International Studies, University of Bath, UK.

Aaron Winter, Criminology, University of East London, UK.

The wreckage of white supremacy

Nasar Meer

> *This is how one pictures the angel of history. His face is turned toward the past. Where we perceive a chain of events, he sees one single catastrophe which keeps piling wreckage upon wreckage and hurls it in front of his feet. The angel would like to stay, awaken the dead, and make whole what has been smashed. But a storm is blowing from Paradise; it has got caught in his wings with such violence that the angel can no longer close them. This storm irresistibly propels him into the future to which his back is turned, while the pile of debris before him grows skyward. This storm is what we call progress.*
>
> Benjamin (1969: 257-58)

Introduction

Walter Benjamin's famous passage from *Illuminations* (Benjamin 1969) is difficult to do justice, but its oracular character is hard to escape. In its prophetic mode, his allegorical angel of history is blown backward through its moment in time and on into a future not of its making; retaining in view the past only as catastrophe at its feet. In our present, flagstones of anti-racism are being upturned and piled high. In this wreckage, fascists are renamed 'populists', white 'racial self-interest' is not racism, and minorities pose a 'demographic challenge'. Frequently, those who govern us make a virtue of this debris and recast it as necessary features of discourse and policy, perhaps as part of 'perform[ing] the problem of totalizing a people' (Bhabha 1994, 160–1). The storm that propels our present wreckage is carried by the force of whiteness, as racial privilege and as supremacy, and just as in Benjamin's time, there is a current of intellectual collusion, in that some social and political scientists have offered 'analytical apologetics for the frank neo-fascism expressed by much of the new populist politics' (Favell, 2019: 159). This is obscured by a sleight of hand: in the name of supposedly value free enquiry, they smuggle a normative cargo that platforms a white majoritarianism. Reliant on a faulty view of the social sciences, in which a subscription to a very narrowly conceived hypothetico-deduction shields them from ethical responsibility, it is empirically dubious because it is philosophically mistaken. At its core, it confuses the *explanadum* with the *explanans*. To frame it in these terms borrows from Hempel and Oppenheim (1948, 152) who wanted to use these terms to understand events 'by virtue of the realization of certain specified antecedent conditions'. In this respect, the explanandum (what is the contemporary provenance of racist 'populist' nationalism?) meets the response of the *explanans* ('the presence of racial minorities'). Any discerning social and political scientist should see this for what it is – an intellectual justification for racism.

By contrast in this special issue, the contributors seek to study the dynamic social and political character of whiteness as privilege and whiteness as supremacy. This simple objective makes for a difficult task. One reason is analytical. As Twine and Gallagher (2008, 10) put it some years ago, social science often struggles to focus 'on the institutions that created, reproduced and normalized white supremacy', concentrating instead on 'the pathology of racist individuals rather than the structural forces that produced racist social systems'. There are exceptions to this of course, especially amongst those informed from by Critical Race Theory and Critical Whiteness Studies traditions surveyed in this special issue. These exceptions recognise that the challenge is not only an analytical narrowness, but the constant reassertion and renewal of racial projects which seek to normalise the different facets of white supremacy, perhaps as what Peter Hervik (this issue) terms a 'fractal logic' – a never ending pattern that recursively feeds itself. It is to both these concerns, the analytical and the political, that the collection of papers in this special issue are oriented. In this very short introduction, and drawing on previously published ideas, I sketch out and re-state some of the historical terrain on which this contribution proceeds.

While all of the papers in this collection are present focused, the issues they address are shaped by a historical character of white supremacy. Of course provenance and continuity are two different things, and for this reason merely noting the objectives of the nineteenth century racial scientists who gave form and content to whiteness is insufficient in explaining present social and political implications, even if it was instructive. This includes physiologists and anthropologists such as Johann Blumenbach, who divided the people of the world into 'Caucasians', 'Mongolians', 'Malayans', 'Negroids' and 'Americans' (First Nations). The 'Caucasian variety', owed its title to Mount Caucasus because 'its southern slope, produces the most beautiful race of men'. Like many of his contemporaries, Blumenbach curated a racial hierarchy in which Northern Europeans were ascendant (Meer 2014).

The fascinating point is that this hierarchy was always fragile, vulnerable under the weight of its own contradictions, and deeply insecure. In his account, Bonnett (2008) excavates an 'ethno-cultural repertoire' of whiteness, and the ways this was given particular content by writers who anxiously debated the 'decline' of white dominance (ibid.: 23). Amongst others, Bonnett (2008) identifies Benjamin Kidd's *Social Evolution* (Kidd 1894) and *Principles of Western Civilisation* (Kidd 1902), each of which prefigure the current theories of European decline (Meer, 2012). Of course, Kidd was writing at a time when the British Empire reigned over nearly a quarter of planet's landmass and people, and alongside other European powers grew wealthy from what they had taken. Pointing to the thesis of the nineteenth-century educationalist and politician Charles Pearson in particular, Bonnett (2008, 18) describes some recurring features in this perception of decline:

> Pearson's principle explanation of why white expansion was at an end and white supremacy in retreat rests on demographics (notably Chinese and African fertility), geographical determinism (the unsuitability of the 'wet tropics' for white settlement) and the deleterious consequences of urbanisation on human 'character'. Moreover, and crucially the economic ascendancy of those who Inge, following Pearson, was later to term 'the cheaper races' (Inge 1922, 27), meant the white 'will be driven from every neutral market and forced to confine himself within his own' (Pearson, 1894: 137).

There is much here which spans several presumed features of culture and civilisation (intertwined in biology and environment), but which is principally underwritten by the ways in which whiteness served as a form of substantive rationality that fashioned geopolitics in its own image. Empire and colonialism are thus understood as natural states of international relations and indicative of human progress. Amongst writers of the day, challenges to this hegemony (and related geopolitical formations) must have raised some profound existential questions. These were certainly evident following the Japanese naval annihilation of the Russian fleet in 1904, where 'for the first time since the Middle Ages, a non-European country had vanquished a European power in a major war' (Mishra 2012, 1).

What is especially interesting is that this violent disruption occurred just at the moment the transaction between Whiteness and the West had been taking place, but in a manner 'in which the mass of white people are treated with suspicion' (Bonnett 2008, 20). This seeming paradox is explained by an internal racial hierarchy that drew upon notions of both race and class and informed what would later become familiar tropes of social Darwinism and eugenicist thinking. This tension, 'of asserting both white solidarity and class elitism was resolved, in part, by asserting that the "best stock" of the working class had long since climbed upwards' (ibid.: 21), and which continued to feed into parallel debates about culture and political economy (McDermott 2006). The especially relevant implications of this genealogy for our discussion in that '[w]hilst "Westerner" can and does sometimes operate as a substitute term for "white", it also operates within new landscapes of power and discrimination that have new and often fragile relationships with the increasingly widely repudiated language of race' (Bonnett 2008, 18).

In another reading, meanwhile, Virdee (2014) has charted the ways in which whiteness during the same period became 'democratised', not least through the expansion of social democratic politics on which pivots a historical seesaw of inclusion and exclusion. It is a dramatic and compelling account in so far as '[e]ach time the boundary of the nation was extended to encompass ever more members of the working class, it was accompanied and legitimised through the further racialization of nationalism that prevented another more recently arrived group from being included' (Virdee, 2014, 5). In this account, race and whiteness were 'constitutive in the making, unmaking and remaking of the working class in England across two centuries' (Virdee 2014: 5–6). As such, and especially in the organisation of social and political life, 'there were historical moments when the working class suppressed such expressions of racism, and on occasion, actively rejected it' (ibid.). Such is the nature of racialization: a juddering movement of the rejection of one group and the incorporation of another (or later indeed the same group), yet which can be quite consistent with intellectual and popular logics of racializing.

These are principally European and imperial trajectories of whiteness of course, and a different account emerges from the north American experience; an account that has been especially compelling for its exploration of whiteness in social relations, specifically what Dyer (1988, 44) once termed as 'seeming not to be anything in particular'. In addition to routinised racial terror, from the US literature in particular, we grasp the paradox which stems from being intimately part of a polity while excluded from its formal story, or, as Du Bois 1999, 10–11) put it, 'being an outcast and stranger in mine own house'. What Du Bois termed 'double consciousness' mediated between agency and structure, individual and society, and between minority and majority subjectivities. It would span the internalisation by African-Americans of the contempt white America had for them, and the creation of an additional perspective in the form of a 'gifted second sight' to which experiencing this gives rise. It would highlight the incongruences emerge from conceiving of African-Americans as having fewer civic rights but no less the duties or responsibilities of an ideal of American citizenship, and the diverging sets of unreconciled ideals or 'strivings' held by African-Americans which are objected to by white society, specifically emerging from an 'enduring hyphenation' signalled in his notion of 'twoness'.

Drawing on this, what the modern US literature emphasises is that white supremacy might be easier to name than the ways in which whiteness serves as what Du Bois termed a public and psychological wage, and what others have termed a 'knapsack' (McIntosh 1988) or 'possessive investment' (Lipstiz 1998). Each of these refer to a kind of capital, and are illustrated in what Duster (2001, 114–15) elaborates as 'deeply embedded in the routine structures of economic and political life. From ordinary service at Denny's restaurants, to far greater access to bank loans to simple police-event-free driving – all these things have come unreflectively with the territory of being white'. In social and political contexts characterised by a hyper-vigilance of non-whites, and as Damian Breen and myself show (this issue) of Muslims in particular, this latent whiteness is often given renewed content through a particular racialization of these groups. Simultaneously, it is sustained by how whiteness is a type of habitus and the norm against which others are judged, in which 'culture and ideology constantly re-cloak whiteness as a normative identity' (ibid.: 12). As Escafre-Dublet (this issue) shows of French cultural policy, white boundary making is embedded in the 'routine structures' of cultural life. She illustrates this through the example of national cultural policy which privileges white majorities and demands that minorities justify the social benefit of any of their artistic initiative. Indeed, the privilege of white majorities is not to have to justify any social benefit – they can pursue art for the sake of it, but minorities have to justify that what they do is useful (or more specifically, to perform to their integration to French society).

What is also implied here is that individuals do not have to be 'white people' to actively reinforce and act in the interests of whiteness (Ladson-Billings, 1998). Whiteness thus sits at an intersection between historical privilege and identity, something that has a contemporary dynamic but which is not an unbroken history (or can be distant to) how many white people experience their identities. As Frankenberg (2001, 76) puts it 'whiteness as a site of privilege is not absolute but rather cross-cut by a range of other axes of relative advantage and subordination; these do not erase or render irrelevant race privilege, but rather inflect or modify it'. One of the sociological implications of this is that there is a documented tendency amongst 'ethnically ambiguous' minorities to seek the material and symbolic rewards of whiteness by positioning themselves as white in such things as applications for education employment, and other training (Warren and Twine 1997; Lee, 2001). This is evident, argue Twine and Gallagher (2008, 14), in how 'whiteness is continuing to expand in the United States, and that it continues to incorporate ethnics of multiracial, Asian, Mexican and other Latinos of non-European heritage'. The study of whiteness then struggles with a wide front of sociological realities, including forms of innovative anti-racist action discussed by Alana Lentin (this issue). None of this should not be taken to imply a lack of agency to resist amongst those deemed non-white in the past (including people who may be deemed white today), and especially people from the Global South, whether in the metropole or periphery, who mobilised, resisted, remade solidarity and found common cause despite conditions of brutal occupation and cultural denigration (Gopal, 2019).

It is especially implausible then that non-whiteness is laundered from prevailing stories of the working-class. This is different from the concerns that the attribution of a conscious or unwitting white dominance may under-recognise how '[t]he economic and psychological wages of whiteness may be more meagre (and thus more precious) the lower down the social hierarchy the white subject is located' (Garner 2006, 262). Of course, a prevailing danger here, as shown by Mondon and Winter (this issue) is that such framings exclude working-class Black, Minority Ethnic and immigrant experiences, and probationary membership, of this strata. As they elaborate, such representations of the white working-class as left behind, sometimes in the service of racist nationalisms and anti-immigration politics, work together in a form of racialised divide and rule to deny belonging and resources, and reinforce racism and racial inequality. In opening up these readings, Nayak's (Nayak 2003a, 2003b) research has utilised ethnographic methods in post-industrial settings in order to explore how whiteness intersects with class and masculinities, and so is negotiated in ways that takes on 'multiple and contingent' meanings (Nayak 2003a, 319). This is especially evident in terms of how 'young people inhabit white ethnicities to different degrees and with varying consequences' (ibid.) not least because 'whiteness is not simply constituted in relation to blackness, but is also fashioned *through and against other versions of whiteness*' (ibid.: 320, emphasis added). What this emphasises is that whiteness is curated and sustained by much more than imperial legacies (Meer 2018).

Of course, and to restate the argument I have made previously, this does not mean uncoupling whiteness from race writ large. On the contrary, the challenge is to get a sense of how that manifests itself in contemporary social processes. As Leonard (this issue) puts it, 'whiteness not only continues to deliver entitlements but, in multiple contexts and political moments, is demonstrating a "backlash" against the assumed gains of non-white Other'. Uncoupling power in the name of complexity, however, is a prominent feature of some contemporary discussion. Perhaps then in thinking about white supremacy we need to connect the two slightly different frames. By supremacy what is meant is dominance, explicitly as coercion but also implicitly through kinds of prevailing consensus amongst white-majority society. Illustrations of the latter include the ways in which once racially segregated societies continue to operate racial zones even while there is no formal policy to support it. Obvious examples are post-Apartheid South Africa and post-Segregation southern states in the US, where racial categories are keenly related to the exercise of power. Yet there are also less obvious examples found in every liberal-democratic European Union state, manifested in the reluctance of visible minorities to move or live outside of urban centres that are often considered much 'safer' than non-urban conurbations (Neal, 2009). This is a different kind of white dominance to that of explicitly white nationalist movements such as the Klu Klux Klan in the US, though of course far right-wing parties in Europe often form part of the political mainstream and may also be in governing coalitions, and look set to feature more.

With their opening paper, Mondon and Winter (this issue) chart a re-emergence and reassertion of white supremacy as a normalised political category, and racism as a legitimate political position across the right of the political spectrum. Using the US and British cases, they discuss the mainstreaming of the far-right and racism with a particular emphasis on the racialisation of the working class as 'people' or 'demos' in the Brexit and Trump campaigns, which not only made race central, but delegitimised Black, minority ethnic and immigrant experiences and interests. Moving to northern Europe and turning to the use of 'fractal logics', as a means to re-think racialization and ideas and practices of whiteness, Hervik (these issues) focuses on the trope of a white 'nation-in-danger'. Found in circulating images, soundbites, visual signs, metaphors, and narratives created in political communication and news media, this discursive portrayal becomes impossible to understand without an account of the prevailing racialization of non-white minorities to whom it is related.

From here a pair of articles discuss whiteness and France. In the first, using ethnographic research amongst France's North African second-generation, Beaman (this issue) discusses how whiteness is at the centre of France's racial project where, as per Omi and Winant's (1994) formulation, differences among individuals are marked without explicit state-sanctioned racial and ethnic categories. In her analysis, and despite an official 'masking' of difference based on France's Republican ideology, the state has an increasingly narrow definition of what it means to be 'French', a definition which often excludes particular populations within French society, including those who were born in France to parents who are immigrants from former French colonies in North Africa. In the second, meanwhile, Escafré-Dublet details how cultural life and the arts re-state an implicit white hegemony. Far from addressing a limited audience in France, cultural policies are an area of definition of a common national culture. They are continuously called upon, she argues, in order to solve identity-related issues such as secularism, religious radicalism or national integration. The prevailing whiteness of this cultural definition is unrecognised even while is serves to establish a universal and unqualified norm.

Part of the dynamic force of white privilege is that in the rare cases it is undeniably explicit, counter-strategies avail themselves to off-set it. How this is negotiated amongst white actors is taken up by Leonard's (this issue) discussion of post-Apartheid south Africa. Her analysis builds on scholarship examining historical processes of readjustment, by drawing on research conducted with a diverse sample of 'white British' who migrated to South Africa in the 1960s, 1970s and 1980s. Her research reveals that amongst British – born residents in South Africa, a range of rhetorical tactics help negotiate a position in relation to both the retreating apartheid regime and the contemporary state. Underpinning the diversity of these subjectivities, a sense of detachment from the nation is demonstrated, and albeit articulated in very different ways, the longstanding identification of the British as 'ambivalent' emerges as a valuable resource by which to excuse an ongoing lack of participatory nationhood in the 'new' South Africa. In the contribution from Breen and myself (this issue), we revisit systems approaches to white privilege and supremacy by returning to Critical Race Theory and tests it explanatory capacity against the contemporary racialization of minorities in Europe, most specifically the experience of British Muslim communities. In a social and political context characterised by a hypervigilance of non-white difference, the article argues that CRT can provide a fruitful means of gauging the ways in which anti-Muslim discrimination might be engendered. This includes the ways in which anti-Muslim discrimination is articulated at the macro level in public discourse and public policy. The article concludes that applying CRT allows us to explore how interest convergence sanctions racialization in context where whiteness and white privilege often run together. Finally, in her closing paper Lentin (this issue) examines a recent arrival in the antiracist toolkit of mobile phone apps for education and intervention, and how this reflects their relation to whiteness as a site for antiracist intervention. Her paper concludes by suggesting a need for wariness around the centring of whiteness in the antiracism struggle, an endeavour which by replicating it, potentially fails in the aim of dismantling white supremacist structures – an objective to which this entire issue is presented.

Acknowledgments

I am very grateful to all the contributors to this special issue, which was first commissioned by Claire Alexander in 2017 before I took up the role of Editor in Chief. A special thanks to Gezim Krazniqi for overseeing the reviewing process, and to Aaron, Angeline, and Jean for helpful comments on this introduction.

Disclosure statement

No potential conflict of interest was reported by the author.

References

Benjamin, W. 1969. *Illuminations*. Edited with an Introduction by Hannah Arendt Translated by Harry Zohn. New York: Schocken.
Bhabha, H., ed. 1994. *The Location of Culture*. London: Routledge.
Bonnett, A. 2008. "Whiteness and the West." In *New Geographies of Race and Racism*, edited by C. Dwyer and C. Bressey, 17–28. Aldershot: Ashgate.
Du Bois, W. E. B. 1999. *The Souls of Black Folk*. Critical edition. Critical edition. H. L. Gates Jr & T. H. Oliver. (Eds.). New York, NY: Norton (Original work published 1903).
Duster, T. 2001. "The "morphing" of Properties of Whiteness." In *The Making and Unmaking of Whiteness*, edited by B. B. Rasmussen, E. Klinenberg, I. Nexica, and M. Wray, 113–137. Durham: Duke University Press.
Dyer, R. 1988. "White." *Screen* 29 (4): 44–65. doi:10.1093/screen/29.4.44.
Favell, A. 2019. "Brexit: A Requiem for The Post-national Society?." *Global Discourse* 9 (1): 157-173.

Frankenberg, R. 2001. "The Mirage of an Unmarked Whiteness." In *The Making and Unmaking of Whiteness*, edited by B. B. Rasmussen, E. Klinenberg, I. Nexica, and M. Wray, 72–96. Durham: Duke University Press.

Garner, S. 2006. "The Uses of Whiteness: What Sociologists Working on Europe Can Draw from US Work on Whiteness." *Sociology* 40 (2): 257–275. doi:10.1177/0038038506062032.

Gopal, P. 2019. *Insurgent Empire: Anticolonialism and the Making of British Dissent*. London: Verso.

Hempel, C. G., and P. Oppenheim. 1948. "Studies in the Logic of Explanation." *Philosophy of Science* 15 (2): 135–175. doi:10.1086/286983.

Kidd, B. 1894. *Social Evolution*. London: Macmillan.

Kidd, B. 1902. *Principles of Western Civilization*. London: Macmillan.

Lee, S. 2001. *Using New Racial Categories in the 2000 Census*. Baltimore, MD: Annie E. Casey Foundation.

Lipstiz, G. 1998. *The Possessive Investment in Whiteness: How White People Profit from Identity Politics*. Philadelphia: Temple University Press.

McDermott, M. 2006. *Working-Class White: the Making and Unmaking of Race Relations*. Berkeley: University of California Press.

McIntosh, P. (1988) "White Privilege and Male Privilege: a Personal Account of Coming to See Correspondences through Work in Women's Studies". Working Paper #189, Wellesley: Wellesley College Center for Research on Women. MA 02181. doi: 10.3168/jds.S0022-0302(88)79586-7

Meer, N. 2012. "Misrecognising Muslim Consciousness in Europe." *Ethnicities* 12 (2): 178-197.

Meer, N. 2014. *Race and Ethnicity*. London: Sage.

Meer, N. 2018. "Race and Postcolonialism: Should One Come before the Other?" *Ethnic and Racial Studies* 46 (1): 1163–1181. doi:10.1080/01419870.2018.1417617.

Mishra, P. 2012. *From the Ruins of Empire*. London: Allen Lane.

Nayak, A. 2003a. "'ivory Lives': Economic Restructuring and the Making of Whiteness in a Post-industrial Youth Community." *European Journal of Cultural Studies* 6 (3): 305–325. doi:10.1177/13675494030063003.

Nayak, A. 2003b. "Last of the "real Geordies"? White Masculinities and the Subcultural Response to Deindustrialisation." *Environment and Planning D: Society and Space* 21 (1): 7–25. doi:10.1068/d44j.

Neal, S. 2009. *Rural Identities: Ethnicity and Community in the English Countryside*. Farnham: Ashgate.

Omi, M., and H. Winant. 1994. *Racial Formation in the United States*. New York: Routledge & Kegan Paul.

Pearson, C. 1894. *National Life and Character: A Forecast*. London: Macmillan.

Twine, F., and C. Gallagher. 2008. "The Future of Whiteness: a Map of the 'third Wave'." *Ethnic and Racial Studies* 31 (1): 4–24. doi:10.1080/01419870701538836.

Virdee, S. 2014. *With Racism, Class and the Racialized Outsider*. Basingstoke: Palgrave.

Warren, J., and F. W. Twine. 1997. "White Americans, the New Minority? Non-blacks and the Ever-expanding Boundaries of Whiteness." *Journal of Black Studies* 28 (2): 200–218. doi:10.1177/002193479702800204.

Whiteness, populism and the racialisation of the working class in the United Kingdom and the United States

Aurelien Mondon and Aaron Winter

ABSTRACT
The election of Donald Trump and the Brexit vote were widely hailed as examples of (white) working class revolts. This article examines the populist racialisation of the working class as white and 'left behind', and representative of the 'people' or 'demos', in the campaigns and commentaries. We argue that such constructions made race central, obscured the class make-up, allowed for the re-assertion of white identity as a legitimate political category and legitimised, mainstreamed and normalised racism and the far right. Moreover, it delegitimised Black, Minority Ethnic and immigrant experiences and interests, including working class ones. We show that the construction of the votes as (white) working class revolts, and representing the 'people' and/or 'demos', is based on a partial reading of electoral data, misrepresents the votes, stigmatises the working class, and supports an ideological purpose which maintains the racial, political and economic status quo.

While much of the west has witnessed a resurgence of the far right since the end of the 2000s, 2016 marked a new step in the mainstreaming of reactionary and particularly racist, Islamophobic and xenophobic political movements, agendas and discourses (Mondon and Winter 2017). Amongst others, the Brexit victory in the United Kingdom and Donald Trump's election to the Presidency in the United States have demonstrated that these movements, agendas and discourses can now win key electoral battles. While much has already been written on these two cases and events, the aim of this article is to focus the discussion on the construction of the white working class to promote racist agendas, adding to a limited, but growing analysis (Bhambra 2017, Emejulu 2016, Lentin 2017, Mondon 2017, Nadeem et al. 2017, Saini 2017, Virdee and McGeever 2017, Winter 2017). Our contribution and aim is three-fold: first, to interrogate the construction of these votes, specifically as white working class revolts; second, demonstrate that the prevalent mainstream explanations about the rise of a (white) working class reaction is based on an ideological racialised construction of the working class and skewed reading of data in both cases that do not sustain even basic scrutiny; third, that such explanations and skewered data reproduce and even support a particular discourse and political agenda, legitimising Trump and Brexit, as well as racism and xenophobia, and delegitimising the working class, whether consciously or not.

To achieve so, this article examines this mainstreaming of racism, focusing on the transformation of the discourses and rhetoric about race and class. Particular attention is paid to the populist racialisation of the working class as white and indigenous in the Brexit and Trump campaigns. In doing so, the aim of this article is not to explain the reasons behind the vote for Trump or Brexit, but rather to examine such explanations and how these reproduce or even support a particular discourse and political agenda. The first section provides some context to highlight and examine the ways in which Brexit and the election of Trump were constructed as working class revolts in mainstream elite and populist discourse, essentialising the working class as white (but also predominantly male), and positing it as a reactionary proxy for the embodiment of the 'people' and, following from this, these votes as a reactionary proxy for revolution. To challenge such a deeply anchored narrative, the article takes a two-pronged approach: first, it demonstrates that the construction of these events as working class revolts, ignores the diversity of the working class to promote an essentialist narrative based on white identity, experience and interests. The article then moves on to challenge the fact that these votes were in fact working class by examining voting patterns and results and highlighting that such claims rest not only on exaggerations, but ideological assumptions and political agendas which reaffirm the campaigns. Finally, the article discusses the implications of such constructions, claims and narratives and how they reproduce, reaffirm or even support particular political discourses and agendas based in pre-existing power and privilege.

White working class revolt(s)?

In October 2016, as the US election loomed, Farage (2016) wrote in an opinion piece in *The Telegraph*, a symbol of his media prominence:

> The similarities between the different sides in this election are very like our own recent battle. As the rich get richer and big companies dominate the global economy, voters all across the West are being left behind. The blue-collar workers in the valleys of South Wales angry with Chinese steel dumping voted Brexit in

their droves. In the American rust belt, traditional manufacturing industries have declined, and it is to these people that Trump speaks very effectively....

This kind of statements was not limited to far-right politicians claiming political support from the working class, but had become common in much of the political commentary in 2016. To provide key context, the aim of this section is to present and examine a selection of statements and analyses from political actors, the media and intellectuals to illustrate the way in which Brexit and Trump's election were constructed as working class revolts. For *The New Statesman*, Trump and Brexit were 'a working class revolt' (Crampton 2016). In March 2016, Fox News called Trump 'the working-class candidate' (Fox News 2016). In the UK, *The Daily Express* talked about a 'working class revolution' (Gutteridge 2016) and Spiked! (2016) claimed 'The Brexit vote was a revolt against the establishment', its editor arguing that argued that 'Britain's poor and workless have risen up' (O'Neill 2016). In *The Guardian*, John Harris (2016) claimed that 'Britain is in the midst of a working-class revolt". In *The New York Times*, David Brooks (2016) referred to Trump's election as a 'revolt of the masses', while Cohn (2016) claimed that Trump 'won working class whites'.

Much of the narrative which followed both the election of Trump and Brexit has been based on murky definitional grounds: the so-called 'working class' is usually painted as the socio-economically and politically disenfranchised and alienated, but also as essentially white and indigenous. This allows it to become at once particular as 'white' and 'working class' and universal as the 'people' or 'demos' (for the latter, see Todd 2015). While the populist character of the campaigns and their portrayal in the mainstream media pitted a constructed 'people' made up of workers against an out-of-touch or contemptuous elite who fails to represent them, its nativist/racist/xenophobic basis pitted whites against classless immigrants, refugees and representatives of multiculturalism and diversity who threaten jobs, resources and nation. For Virdee and McGeever (2017) 'This racializing nationalism has borne a particularly defensive character since the 2008 crisis. It is defined not by imperial prowess or superiority, but by a deep sense of loss of prestige; a retreat from the damaging impact of a globalized world that is no longer recognizable, no longer British'. This operates through what has been described by Song (2014) as a culture of racial equivalence: this 'post-race' narrative does not negate race or racism, but allows for the discursive placement of whiteness in a position where it has lost its historical power (globally and domestically) and appears thus in decline, vulnerable and subject to victimisation by others.[1] This narrative and the identification of whiteness with the working class, negates its privilege and renders it the 'people'.

In the UK, while the Conservative-led Vote Leave was the official campaign for Brexit, the UKIP-led Leave.EU received much coverage as Nigel Farage had been instrumental in leading the agenda on the issue since the 2014 European election. The nationalist argument was central to the campaign as demonstrated by its slogan: 'We want our country back: VOTE TO LEAVE ON 23RD JUNE'. For Farage, Brexit was a victory for 'ordinary people, for good people, for decent people' (Peck 2016), one which confirmed that concerns over immigration, as well as Islam, came first and economic grievances second (Hall and Maddox 2016). Often, the Leave.EU campaign tapped into far right strategies, most notably with its use of a Nazi-esque image of refugees crossing from Croatia to Slovenia in 2015, with a banner reading 'Breaking Point: the EU has failed us all' (Stewart and Mason 2016). It was therefore not surprising to see the far right rally behind Farage (Lyons 2016).

Trump's campaign was similar to Leave.EU, and UKIP's more generally, and targeted post-industrial 'red states' traditionally associated with conservative white working-class constituencies, combining protectionist rhetoric with anti-immigration tropes. His slogan, 'Make America Great Again' was a nod to an idealised industrial period of plentiful jobs, economic security and implied cultural security, but also a dog whistle to nostalgia for a pre-PC, pre-affirmative action and even pre-civil rights era when white men ruled unchallenged. As Anderson (2016, 161) points out, less than a month after Dylann Roof killed nine African-Americans at Emanuel African Methodist Episcopal Church in Charleston, South Carolina, Trump told an audience at a GOP nomination rally 'Don't worry, we'll take our country back'. On election day, he declared: 'Today the American working class is going to strike back, finally' (Cohn 2016). Trump's nostalgia and assertions that he and his target base would take back the country and strike back, linked to his racist, Islamophobia and xenophobic rhetoric and proposed policies to do this, racialised the working class as white, with a right to the nation's past and future over others. This made it unsurprising that he received endorsements from the far right. This included Rocky Suhayda of the American Nazi Party, Don Black of Stormfront (Neiwert and Posner 2016), 'Alt-Right' figurehead Richard Spencer and former Grand Wizard of the Ku Klux Klan David Duke, as well as more mainstream right-wing gateway figures and white nationalist enablers from Breitbart such as Steve Bannon and Milo Yiannopoulos (Winter 2017, 2018).

While the far right in both the US and UK benefitted from the racialisation of the working class, it was more surprisingly taken up by part of the left, who made tackling immigration a key issue (Wearing 2017; Bush 2015; Travis 2009). For Labour MP Emma Reynolds, the message was clear: 'Trump and Brexit show that progressives cannot take white working-class voters for granted'. A number of academic analyses also participated in either reproducing, constructing or informing the narrative. Arguments about the white working class 'left-behind' became common to explain the resurgence of far right parties as it was argued right-wing populist were able to attract former left-wing voters alienated by the convergence of the mainstream left and right and their focus on the middle class. According to Ford and Goodwin (2017), support for Brexit is to be found within the working-class 'left-behind' who fear a loss of order and identity in 'a more diverse and rapidly changing Britain', championed by a homogenised and mythologised social liberal elite. A similar argument was developed by Goodhart (2013) who argued that increased diversity, through mass immigration, threatened social solidarity for the 'somewhere' in opposition to the rootless, socially liberal, middle-class, cosmopolitan 'anywhere' Goodhart (2017).

In the US, Vance (2017) argues that one must look at the economic and cultural crisis of the white working and underclass in rural America to understand Trump's support and victory. Hochschild (2016) foregrounds the 'cultural' in terms of race, gender and sexuality, arguing that, 'To white, native-born, heterosexual men, ... [Trump] offered a solution to the dilemma they had long faced as the 'left-behinds' of the 1960s and 1970s celebration of other identities. As Bhambra (2017) argued, 'methodological whiteness' has distorted social scientific analysis of Brexit and Trump: '[t]he politics of both campaigns was also echoed in those social scientific analyses that sought to focus on the "legitimate" claims of the "left behind" or those who had come to see themselves as "strangers in their own land"', as Hochschild phrases it, both racialised as white. This, we argue, not only accepts but legitimises the narrative of loss, disenfranchisement and victimisation, but also that of its original entitlement and the nationalism and racism that underpins and flows from it. This trend in academia is not new. As Hill (2004; 9) suggested, 'Recent scholarship on race has increasingly turned into the historical pressures now besetting the fiction Americans still insist on calling the white race. In doing so, it has marked the same attention to whiteness that made it possible for AR's [American Renaissance's] men to echo'. It was at AR that Hill (2004, 5–6) met the BNP's Nick Griffin who was targeting the white working-class vote in Britain at that time, notably in post-industrial former labour strongholds, before UKIP replaced them.

The assumption that the alienation suffered by the white working class has translated into a strong opposition to immigration and diversity has led some commentators to argue that the liberal elite's reaction and general anti-racist attitudes are in fact contempt towards the democratic voice of 'ordinary people'. This was expressed by Kaufmann (2017) in his report *'Racial self-interest' is not racism* where he argued that Brexit was an expression of white, particularly working class, racial self-interest (what Goodhart terms 'White Identity Politics'). For Kaufmann, it is crucial to 'avoid using charges of racism to side-line discussions of ethno-demographic interests' in relation to issues such as opposition to immigration. According to Goodhart, cited in the report, 'The liberal reflex to tar legitimate majority grievances with the brush of racism risks deepening western societies' cultural divides'.

The conflation of anti-racism and elitism, and the representation of the white working class as the victims of elite anti-racism which slips between racialised classism and reverse racism is also central to the libertarian right's approach to Brexit and Trump. Online magazine *Spiked!* has been particularly active in developing this line of argumentation. As Furedi (2016) declared:

> In the eyes of too many Remain strategists, the uneducated working classes have few redeeming qualities. They were frequently portrayed as parochial xenophobes who hate immigrants, who hold on to outdated values, and who fear uncertainty and change. In the aftermath of the referendum, the hatred directed at 'those people' … has intensified.).

Such argumentation is often accompanied by articulations and justifications of alleged working-class concerns about immigration and limits on free speech, most notably so-called 'political correctness'. Like Furedi, Milo Yiannopoulos (2017) claimed that 'Liberals have lots of theories for why working class whites abandoned them. The most obvious of which is their old standby, "they are racist"'. It is frequently framed as a response to commentators who express concern about a link between Brexit, Trump and racism, while it is in fact the response itself which reifies the link. This in turn places the blame squarely on the working class rather than on the campaigns, the way they are covered and the diversity of supporters.

Pushed to its extreme, this argument both served to delegitimise well-documented evidence of spikes in far-right activities and racist attacks created by the referendum and the US election by making it about elite classism (Weaver 2016; Travis 2016; Hatewatch Staff 2016a, 2016b; Farmer 2017; Hatewatch Staff 2017; Miller and Werner 2016). *Spiked!*'s Luke Gittos (2016) claimed that 'the onset of panic has revealed how the very publications and commentators who once claimed to stand up for the working class in fact view working-class people as a violent, racist horde'. In these cases, the commentators ignore the mainstreaming of racism and it is themselves who seem to think that the working class is white, are responsible for Brexit and Trump, speak as or for the people and democracy, and are the target of accusations of racism. To explore this further, we now move to examine and challenge the concept of whiteness and construction of the white working class, as well as such narratives.

Who are the (white) working class?

This section examines and interrogates the concept, construction and narrative of the white working-class revolt around Brexit and Trump. There is no doubt that the working class in Britain and America faces great inequality in a post-industrial context following the 2010 economic crisis, growing neoliberal policies, deregulation, housing crises, austerity in the UK, and an opioid epidemic in the US. That said, the racialised construction of the working class as white, or merely the focus on the 'white working class', in revolt against the establishment presents a number of issues. The first, is the fact that the working class is not white and that the socio-economic inequality and political disenfranchisement they experience is also experienced, often to a greater degree, by Black and Minority Ethnic working class people. This construction and narrative thus ignores this intersectionality, white privilege and the effects of such racialised divide and rule on communities. It is a distraction from an actual anti-establishment critique of and revolt against entrenched power. Linked to this, the white working class is subject to historically contingent definitions of whiteness and racialised or ethnicised divisions (e.g. Jewish, Polish and Irish Catholic), often around immigration, labour and reactionary political movements and ideologies. Thirdly, if we consider that the working class being discussed is only white and the fact that the Trump and Brexit campaigns were led by figureheads from elite and establishment backgrounds, such as Trump, Farage and Boris Johnson, as well as discourses of general white and national decline, it appears that it was whiteness, national identification and indigenous status that was at stake as opposed to socio-economic status or class.

According to Virdee (in Patel 2015),

> *so much of the history and sociology of the working class of Britain had failed to integrate the experiences of the racialized fractions within this working class – the Irish Catholics, Jews, Asians and Caribbeans. It was almost as if the working assumption of these academics and socialist historians was that the working class was wholly white.*

In *Race, Class and the Racialised Outsider*, Virdee (2014) examines the ways in which racialised groups immigrated to Britain, were targeted racially and scapegoated, joined the working class and were central to working class history, the development of British industry, and the negotiation of both Britishness and whiteness. He argues that Jewish and Irish working-class subjects are particularly instructive: having entered the working class as racialised immigrant groups, they 'became' white, demonstrating the contingency of the concept of whiteness.

The working class in the US has been shaped through a history of slavery and racism, immigration and specifically both external and internal labour migration (e.g. from Chinese rail workers, the migration of African-Americans from the Jim Crow South to the industrial North, and Mexican labourers) which informs a racialised class system and diverse working class. As a white settler colony, and while all white people come from elsewhere, some are whiter than others. Ignatiev (1995, 1996); Frye Jacobson (1998) and Roediger (1999) have all looked at whiteness as historical, contingent and constructed. Through their study of

European migration to the United States, they have demonstrated how Jews, Irish Catholics, Southern Italians and Greeks were racialised and excluded from whiteness, but eventually became white (a concept Jacobson terms 'probationary whiteness'), through various historical processes, racial/racist differentiation, new waves of immigration and leaving the working class. Roediger (1999) argues that such groups only became white, in the Anglo-American sense, by distinguishing themselves from Black slaves and freemen, including in labour market competition. For Ignatiev (1996), the ability for them to become white Americans was linked to buying property outside the industrial working class cities and ghettos. This was not something afforded to African-Americans, Asians and Hispanic people.

Returning to the present context, the construction and mobilisation of the white working class around Brexit did not go unnoticed or unchallenged. For the Runnymede Trust (Khan and Shaheen 2017), the racialisation of the working class and focus on white interests ignored the wider diversity of the working class and inequality faced by Black and minority ethnic communities, migrants and refugees. This divide and rule politics constructed a zero-sum competition for representation and reduced resources between the 'indigenous' white working class and 'others', even though socio-economic inequality and related problems (poverty, lack of social mobility, low wages, housing and institutional representation), predominantly represented as white working class problems, 'cut across racial groups', with ethnic minorities suffering the brunt of austerity politics (Khan 2017; see also Runnymede Trust 2015). Bassel and Emejulu (2017a, 2017b) also demonstrate the disproportionate effect of austerity on women of colour in their research on Britain and France. The gender aspect is important due to the fact that in the 'left behind' discourse, the post-industrial working class is not only presumed to be white, but male. White men are posited as having lost their jobs, earning power, status and ability to support and protect their family and maintain their patriarchal and masculine power.

This can be seen in the ways in which Brexit rhetoric intersected with fears of Muslims and particularly refugees threatening British women and children and the ways in which Trump's support intersected with anti-feminist, men's rights and anti-PC sexist rhetoric. The latter of which was also linked to opposition to Hillary Clinton's campaign. Support and voting patterns also highlight gender issues, particularly in relation to race, which we will return to in section three. In the United States, while de-industrialisation and recession hurt the 'rust-belt' and 'red states' (code for white working class), Black and Hispanic people remained more likely to live in poorer neighbourhoods than white people with working class incomes (Goyette and Scheller 2016). Between 2007 and 2010 (recession), Hispanic wealth fell by 44%, and black wealth by 31%, compared to 11% for white families, and it was Black people who were more likely to be targeted and affected by subprime mortgages (Eisenbrey 2014).

In contrast with this diversity, leaders of these movements were predominantly white, but not working class. The gap between the rhetoric and reality was made clearest when Farage and Trump, two wealthy businessmen, were pictured in a gold elevator in Trump Tower (Withnall 2016). Furthermore, cruder acts of racism regularly take place beyond the working class, as was the case with Rhodri Philipps, the 4th Viscount St Davids convicted in June 2017, for threatening and racist Facebook posts directed at prominent anti-Brexit activist Gina Miller and another man of immigrant background (BBC 2017). It is not surprising that this took place in a climate where newspapers owned by wealthy white men declared judges to be 'enemies of the people' for allowing MPs to have a say on triggering article 50 (Phipps 2016).

Finally, despite claims by the campaigns and commentators that these votes were expressions of working class alienation and disenfranchisement, the focus of the campaigns was immigration, Islamophobia and national culture (often code for white), rather than jobs and economics. As previously noted, economics only came coupled with protectionist racism and xenophobia: 'it was cultural anxiety – feeling like a stranger in America, supporting the deportation of immigrants, and hesitating about educational investment' that best predicted white working class support for Trump (Green 2017). It was therefore white racist and not working class interests which were at stake. This raises the question which is the focus of the next section, who actually voted for Brexit and Trump and do they represent the working class and/or revolts?

Brexit and Trump: working-class revolutions?

In the previous section, we interrogated the construction of the 'white working class' historically, conceptually and sociologically. In this section, we test the mainstream narrative further by examining whether Brexit and Trump were indeed propelled by a white working-class revolt. Building on existing research (Runnymede Trust 2017), this section aims to demonstrate that while there is no denying that part of the working class did vote for Trump and Brexit, the mainstream narrative has exaggerated the importance of this vote, and downplayed other demographics such as race and gender.

Despite widespread coverage, claims that Brexit was a working-class revolt are untenable when looking at the geography of the vote. As demonstrated by Dorling (2016) and Sayer (2017), Brexit supporters were mostly found in the wealthier parts of the UK, with 52% of leave voters being from southern half of England. Were it simply a question of class *qua* income for example, Scotland

(62% remain) and Northern Ireland (55.8% remain), whose gross disposable income is lower than the UK's average would have been fertile ground for Brexit.

Analysis in terms of class provides further caveats to the working class revolt. While the 'social grades' categories of the National Readership Survey (2008) are notoriously problematic (see Rubin et al. 2014), they remain the best tools at our disposal, but more importantly those used to create the narratives we are challenging. Using these and including abstention as a variable allows us to weaken such generalising claims further. Unfortunately, the Ashcroft poll (Lord 2016) does not provide estimates regarding abstention per social class, but applying the data available for the 2015 General Election regarding participation, while not ideal, raises some interesting caveats, the most obvious being the ignorance of abstention as an important vector in our democracies (Mondon 2017). The following results were thus calculated based on a similar rate of abstention within each, but adjusted with the overall turnout (27.8% vs 33.9%). With abstention taken into account, the difference between social classes is far less convincing as DE and C2 register a lower turnout than C1 and AB, leading the gap between C2 (42.34%) and AB (35.15%) to narrow from 21% to just 7%. With this calculation, the difference between C1 (38.25%) and DE (39.76%) becomes marginal, thus negating the working-class nature of the vote. This differential between classes is further negated when taking into account the size of each of these social classes within the entire population (see Figure 1): AB (9.49%) and C1 (11.12%) become the largest purveyors of vote for Leave, above both C2 (9.02%) and DE (9.14%) (for more detail, see Mondon 2017, see also Dorling 2016). This more nuanced picture disproves further the idea that the poor/working class/ordinary people rose up against the well-off/elite.[2]

The picture is not dissimilar in the United States where the mainstream narrative about Trump's victory can also be nuanced. An analysis of the exit polls conducted by Edison Research for the National Election Pool (New York Times 2017) does indeed point to a strong performance of Trump with

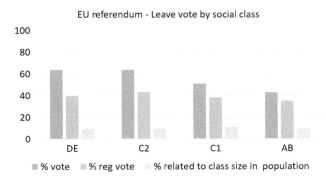

Figure 1. Leave vote per social class. source (Lord 2016, Ipsos Mori 2015, Mondon 2017).

poorly educated white men (see Tables 1 and 2). Compared to the data from 2012, the shift in terms of vote by income is also striking with a much lower gap between Clinton and Trump within the two lower categories, although it must be noted that the Democrat candidate still received a majority of the vote in these categories traditionally associated with the working-class. However, what is particularly interesting here, and conspicuously absent in much of the media coverage about the white working class revolt, is to compare Trump's support with that of previous Republican candidates. While Trump did appeal to poorer voters in larger numbers than Mitt Romney or John McCain, his performance was similar to George Bush Jr's, thus suggesting that this may not be the working-class breakthrough widely advertised.

The same seems to be true about education. Romney and McCain did particularly poorly against Obama within the least educated voter categories, making Trump's appeal within these categories appear like a real breakthrough. However, Trump's performance is again far less exceptional when compared to Bush's in 2004.

Finally, Trump's performance with white voters is certainly strong, but again does not appear to be significantly different from previous Republican candidates (see Table 3).

There is no denying however that Trump managed to appeal to more less-educated white men than his predecessors. While Bush and Romney appealed to 61% of the 'white without a college degree electorate', McCain 58%, Trump appealed to 67% of that category. Yet Trump's 'breakthrough' is further nuanced by Kilibarda and Roithmayr (2016) analysis of the 'myth of the rust belt revolt'

Table 1. Vote in presidential election according to income.

	Size of category in 2016	2016 Clinton	2016 Trump	2012 Obama	2012 Romney	2008 Obama	2008 McCain	2004 Kerry	2004 Bush
Under $30,000	17%	53%	41%	63%	35%	65%	32%	60%	40%
$30,000 – $49,999	19%	51%	42%	57%	42%	55%	43%	50%	49%
$50,000 – $99,999	31%	46%	50%	46%	52%	49%	49%	44%	56%
$100,000 – $199,999	24%	47%	48%	44%	54%	48%	51%	42%	57%
$200,000 or more	10%	47%	49%	44%	54%	52%	46%	35%	63%

Table 2. Vote in presidential election according to level of education.

	Size of category in 2016	2016 Clinton	2016 Trump	2012 Obama	2012 Romney	2008 Obama	2008 McCain	2004 Kerry	2004 Bush
Some college/associate degree	32%	43%	52%	49%	48%	51%	47%	46%	54%
College graduate	32%	49%	45%	47%	51%	50%	48%	46%	52%
Postgraduate study	18%	58%	37%	55%	42%	58%	40%	55%	44%
High school graduate	18%	45%	51%	51%	48%	52%	46%	47%	52%
No high school diploma				64%	35%	63%	35%	50%	49%

Table 3. Vote in presidential election according to level of race.

	Size of category in 2016	2016 Clinton	2016 Trump	2012 Obama	2012 Romney	2008 Obama	2008 McCain	2004 Kerry	2004 Bush
White	70%	37%	58%	39%	59%	43%	55%	41%	58%
Black	12%	88%	8%	93%	6%	95%	4%	88%	11%
Hispanic/Latino	11%	65%	29%	71%	27%	67%	31%	53%	44%
Asian	4%	65%	29%	73%	26%	62%	35%	56%	44%
Other	3%	56%	37%	58%	38%	66%	31%	54%	40%

which demonstrates that Clinton actually lost more 'white working class' votes on Obama than Trump gained on Romney in 2012 (see also Henley 2016). It is also worth noting that Trump won the majority of white professional males with a college education and over 40% of white professional females with a college education, pointing further to race or 'whiteness' over class as a key factor, something which is traditional in the Republican vote. This is backed up by a Public Religion Research Institute survey that showed Trump's appeal could better be explained by a fear of cultural displacement (such as the loss of white male Christian privilege) than real or feared economic displacement (Chokshi 2018).

Interestingly, responses to supplementary questions in the exit poll suggest that, beyond the traditional Republican electorate or middle and upper class conservatives, Trump managed to appeal to a similar electorate than that which has underpinned the resurgence of the far right in Europe. This particular electorate feels insecure about its future, even though it remains in a relatively privileged position and is more interested about issues such as immigration and terrorism, than about the economy. Therefore, rather than a radical shift of the working class towards Trump, what we have witnessed is the development of a typical far right electorate by European standards (see amongst others Crépon, Dézé, and Mayer 2015, Rydgren 2013). While this is certainly a concerning development, the size of this particular electorate is marginal, and would not have been sufficient for Trump to win if the Democrats had managed to retain their share of the vote. A more significant finding is that the largest share of Trump's electorate does not appear to differ from traditional Republican voters, and particularly from Bush's. This means that Trump is more the confirmation of a trend which has seen a radicalisation of the Republican electorate, with racism being increasingly normalised in American politics, and the resurgence of the far right rather than a real break from politics as usual.

Misusing class and its implications

The first part of this article highlighted the way in which mainstream political discourse constructed a narrative around Brexit and Trump's election as white working-class revolts. To challenge this narrative, we have used a two-pronged approach: first, we demonstrated that there is a long history of whitening the working class and ignoring its diversity, thus promoting an essentialist narrative based on white (male) experience. This led us to conclude that, while racism is indeed present in the working class, its diverse nature should not be ignored and the racism present in upper classes should not be downplayed, particularly when the so-called revolt is led by the privileged (both in terms of race and wealth). We then took a more electoral approach and demonstrated that the working class revolts for both Trump and Brexit were in fact far less obvious than the coverage of both electoral contests showed. The working-class nature of these two votes is marginal and can be challenged.

Therefore, we see the white working class narrative as problematic in four ways. The first is that it racialises the working class as white and pits an elusive 'white working class' against racialised minorities and immigrants, who are denied working class status, in a competition for scarce, deregulated and casualised employment and ever dwindling resources in neo-liberal Britain and America. Second, it constructs the 'white working class' as privileging their racial interests above class ones and as being racist, which results in the very stigma right-wing populist and libertarian advocates, who are themselves often part of the elites, falsely and opportunistically claim to oppose. Third, it normalises and mainstreams racism in both discourse and practice by portraying it as a popular demand, thus potentially fuelling hate crime. Finally, in addition to not addressing the inequality faced by 'white' working class people, it exacerbates the inequality and vulnerability faced by racialised and migrant working class peoples and actually serves establishment political and economic interests.

This framing of Brexit and Trump as working class revolts also informed the ways in which responses and reactions to them were constructed. The reaction with regard to the role played by the working class in the events has tended to be split into two distinct camps: those celebrating the working class revolts, and those lamenting the rise of racism within this part of the population. While there is no denying that racist sentiment is on the rise within the working class and that many voted for Trump and Brexit for this reason, our analysis has demonstrated that the working class quality of both votes is not evident and that the majority of supporters for the nativist option came from better off sections of the population traditionally associated with the middle class. The white working class revolt narrative mobilised by the populist far right and hyped by elite discourse (Glynos & Mondon 2016) has ignored not only elite driven racism (e.g. in politics, academia and the media) as well as the more structural, institutional and systemic operation of racism in our societies. For the US, this is supported by the analysis undertaken by Metzgar (2016) and Hubbs (2014) that 'class-based blame-shifting ("It's not us, it's them!") actually supports racist and other systems of oppression'. While those in positions of power (whether political or discursive) have often argued that they are merely responding to what 'the people' want, they have carefully ignored or downplayed the role they play as gate-keepers and shapers of public discourse and their proven influence as agenda-setters. Therefore, rather than 'the people' suddenly reverting to racist attitudes, we argue that it is the widespread and widely publicised acceptance, based on skewed evidence, that 'the people' has turned racist, that perversely led to the legitimisation of a racism as it began to be discussed as a popular feeling, rather than a construction fuelled by elite discourse.

Disclosure statement

No potential conflict of interest was reported by the authors.

Notes

1. For more on the post-racial white backlash, see: Hughley (2014) and Winter (2018).
2. There has also been some attention paid to Brexit voting from within BAME communities. Although it does challenge the 'white working class' Brexit narrative, we are not examining it as the focus of this section is white working class support. It is worth noting though that votes from within these communities is often evoked by Brexiters, along with claims about allowing commonwealth immigration instead of EU immigration post-Brexit, in order to defend against accusations that Brexit was only white and/or racist, but is challenged by racialised nostalgia for Empire, a rise in racist hate incidents and the 2018 Windrush deportation scandal.

ORCID

Aurelien Mondon http://orcid.org/0000-0002-3453-7821
Aaron Winter http://orcid.org/0000-0002-5209-0146

References

Anderson, C. 2016. *White Rage: The Unspoken Truth about Our Racial Divide*. New York: Bloomsbury.
Bassel, L., and A. Emejulu. 2017b. "Whose Crisis Counts? Minority Women, Austerity and Activism in France and Britain." In *Gender and the Economic Crisis in Europe*, edited by J. Kantola, and E. Lombardo, 185-208. London: Palgrave.
Bassel, L., and A. Emejulu. 2017a. *Minority Women and Austerity: Survival and Resistance in France and Britain*. Bristol: Policy Press.
BBC. 2017. "Aristocrat Guilty over "Menacing" Gina Miller Facebook Post." *BBC*, July 11. http://www.bbc.co.uk/news/uk-40574754
Bhambra, G. 2017. "Brexit, Trump, and 'Methodological Whiteness': On the Misrecognition of Race and Class." *British Journal of Sociology: Special Issue on the Trump/Brexit Moment: Causes and Consequences* 68 (S1): S214–S232.
Brooks, D. 2016. "Revolt of the Masses." *New York Times*, June 28. https://www.nytimes.com/2016/06/28/opinion/revolt-of-the-masses.html

Bush, S. 2015. "Labour's Anti-Immigrant Mug: The Worst Part Is, It Isn't a Gaffe." *The New Statesman*, March 28. http://www.newstatesman.com/politics/2015/03/labours-anti-immigrant-mug-worst-part-it-isnt-gaffe

Chokshi, N. 2018. "Trump Voters Driven by Fear of Losing Status, Not Economic Anxiety, Study Finds." *New York Times*, April 24. https://www.nytimes.com/2018/04/24/us/politics/trump-economic-anxiety.html

Cohn, N. 2016. "Why Trump Won Working Class Whites." *New York Times*, November 10. https://www.nytimes.com/2016/11/10/upshot/why-trump-won-working-class-whites.html

Crampton, C. 2016. "Voting for Trump and Brexit: What the Working Class Revolt Is Really About." *The New Statesman*, November 9. http://www.newstatesman.com/world/north-america/2016/11/voting-trump-and-brexit-what-working-class-revolt-really-about

Crépon, S., A. Dézé, and N. Mayer, eds. 2015. *Les Faux-Semblants Du Front National: Sociologie D'un Parti Politique*. Paris: Sciences Po Les Presses.

Dorling, D. 2016. "Brexit: The Decision of a Divided Country." *BMJ* 354. doi:10.1136/bmj.i3697.

Eisenbrey, R. 2014. "Detroit's Bankruptcy Reflects a History of Racism." *Economic Policy Institute*, February 25. http://www.epi.org/blog/detroits-bankruptcy-reflects-history-racism/

Emejulu, A. 2016. "On the Hideous Whiteness of Brexit: "Let Us Be Honest about Our past and Our Present if We Truly Seek to Dismantle White Supremacy"." *Verso Books Blog*, June 28. https://www.versobooks.com/blogs/2733-on-the-hideous-whiteness-of-brexit-let-us-be-honest-about-our-past-and-our-present-if-we-truly-seek-to-dismantle-white-supremacy

Farage, N. 2016. "The Little People Have Had Enough." *The Telegraph*, October 9. http://www.telegraph.co.uk/opinion/2016/10/09/the-little-people-have-had-enough—not-just-here-but-in-america/

Farmer, B. 2017. "Far-Right and neo-Nazi Terror Arrests Double." *The Telegraph*, March 9. http://www.telegraph.co.uk/news/2017/03/09/far-right-neo-nazi-terror-arrests-double/

Ford, R., and M. Goodwin. January, 2017. "Britain After Brexit: A Nation Divided." *Journal of Democracy* 28: 17–30. https://kar.kent.ac.uk/60489/4/Ford_Goodwin_A_Nation_Divided_AAM.pdf

Furedi, F. 2016. "Revolt of the Others." *Spiked*!, June 30. https://www.spiked-online.com/2016/06/30/revolt-of-the-others/

Gittos, L. 2016. "Britain Has Not Become Racist Overnight." *Spiked!* June 28. http://www.spiked-online.com/newsite/article/britain-has-not-become-racist-overnight-brexit-eu/18511#.WN9el_nytPY

Glynos, J., and A. Mondon. 2016. "The Political Logic of Populist Hype: The Case of Right Wing Populism's 'Meteoric Rise' and Its Relation to the Status Quo." Populismus working paper series no. 4.

Goodhart, D. 2013. *The British Dream: Successes and Failures of Post-War Immigration*. London: Atlantic Books.

Goodhart, D. 2017. *The Road to Somewhere: The Populist Revolt and the Future of Politics*. London: C. Hurst.

Goyette, B., and A. Scheller. 2016. "15 Charts That Prove We're Far From Post-Racial". *Huffington Post: Black Voices*, February 7. http://www.huffingtonpost.com/2014/07/02/civil-rights-act-anniversary-racism-charts_n_5521104.html

Green, E. 2017. "It Was Cultural Anxiety that Drove White, Working-Class Voters to Trump." *The Atlantic*, May 9. https://www.theatlantic.com/politics/archive/2017/05/white-working-class-trump-cultural-anxiety/525771/

Gutteridge, N. 2016. "Working Class Revolution? Reports of Huge EU Referendum Turnout Which 'Would Favour Leave'." *The Express*, June 24. http://www.express.co.uk/news/politics/682890/EU-referendum-Reports-huge-EU-referendum-turnout-favour-Leave-Brexit

Hall, M., and D. Maddox 2016. "Nigel Farage Today Warned that Controlling Mass Immigration while Britain Remains in the EU Is Simply Impossible." *The Express*, April 29. http://www.express.co.uk/news/politics/665446/Nigel-Farage-Ukip-control-immigration-leave-EU-referendum-June

Harris, J. 2016. "Britain Is in the Midst of a Working-Class Revolt." *The Guardian*, June 17. https://www.theguardian.com/commentisfree/2016/jun/17/britain-working-class-revolt-eu-referendum doi:10.3310/pgfar04170

Hatewatch Staff. 2016a. "Update: More than 400 Incidents of Hateful Harassment and Intimidation since the Election." *Southern Poverty Law Center*, November 15. https://www.splcenter.org/hatewatch/2016/11/15/update-more-400-incidents-hateful-harassment-and-intimidation-election

Hatewatch Staff. 2016b. "Update: 1094 Bias Related Incidents in the Month following the Election." *Southern Poverty Law Center*, December 16. https://www.splcenter.org/hatewatch/2016/12/16/update-1094-bias-related-incidents-month-following-election

Hatewatch Staff. 2017. "Hate Groups Increase for Second Consecutive Year as Trump Electrifies Radical Right." *Southern Poverty Law Center*, February 15. https://www.splcenter.org/news/2017/02/15/hate-groups-increase-second-consecutive-year-trump-electrifies-radical-right

Henley, J. 2016. "White and Wealthy Voters Gave Victory to Donald Trump, Exit Polls Show." *The Guardian*, November 9. https://www.theguardian.com/us-news/2016/nov/09/white-voters-victory-donald-trump-exit-polls

Hill, M. 2004. *After Whiteness: Unmaking an American Majority*. New York: New York University Press.

Hochschild, A. R. 2016. *Strangers in Their Own Land: Anger and Mourning on the American Right*, 230. New York: New Press.

Hubbs, N. 2014. *Rednecks, Queers, and Country Music*. Jackson: University of California Press.

Hughley, M. W. 2014. "White Backlash in the 'Post-Racial' United States." *Ethnic and Racial Studies* 37 (5): 721–730. doi:10.1080/01419870.2014.886710.

Ignatiev, N. 1995. *How the Irish Became White*. London: Routledge.

Ignatiev, N. 1996. "Immigrants and Whites." In *Race Traitor*, edited by N. Ignatiev, and J. Garvey, 17. London: Routledge.

Ipsos Mori. 2015. *"How Britain Voted in 2015."* London: Ipsos

Jacobson, M. F. 1998. *Whiteness of a Different Colour*. 1998. London: Routledge.

Kaufmann, E. 2017. "Racial Self-Interest Is Not Racism: Ethno-Demographic Interests and the Immigration Debate." *Policy Exchange*, https://policyexchange.org.uk/wp-content/uploads/2017/03/Racial-Self-Interest-is-not-Racism-FINAL.pdf

Khan, O. 2017. "Who Cares About The White Working Class?" *Huff Post UK*, March 21. http://www.huffingtonpost.co.uk/dr-omar-khan/white-working-class-disadvantages_b_15494046.html

Khan, O., and F. Shaheen 2017. "Minority Report: Race and Class in post-Brexit Britain, Runnymede Trust and Class." *Runnymede Trust and CLASS*, March. http://www.

runnymedetrust.org/uploads/publications/pdfs/Race%20and%20Class%20Post-Brexit%20Perspectives%20report%20v5.pdf

Kilibarda, K., and D. Roithmayr. 2016. "The Myth of the Rust Belt Revolt." *Slate*, December 1. http://www.slate.com/articles/news_and_politics/politics/2016/12/the_myth_of_the_rust_belt_revolt.html

Lentin, A. 2017. "On Class and Identity Politics." *Inference Review*. V.3, #2, http://inference-review.com/article/on-class-and-identity-politics

Lord, A. 2016. *How the United Kingdom Voted on Thursday... and Why*. London: Lord Ashcroft Polls. June 24.

Lyons, J. 2016. "Farage Campaign Courted Far Right." *The Sunday Times*, May 22. http://www.thetimes.co.uk/article/farage-campaign-courted-far-right-njrqxhkqb

Metzgar, J. 2016. "Misrepresenting the White Working Class: What the Narrating Class Gets Wrong." *Working Class Perspectives*, March 14. https://workingclassstudies.wordpress.com/2016/03/14/misrepresenting-the-white-working-class-what-the-narrating-class-gets-wrong/

Miller, C., and A. Werner. 2016. "Ten Days After: Harassment and Intimidation in the Aftermath of the Election." *Southern Poverty Law Center*, November 29. https://www.splcenter.org/20161129/ten-days-after-harassment-and-intimidation-aftermath-election

Mondon, A. 2017. "Limiting Democratic Horizons to a Nationalist Reaction: Populism, the Radical Right and the Working Class." *Javnost/The Public: Journal of the European Institute for Communication and Culture* 24 (3): 355-374.

Mondon, A., and A. Winter. 2017. "Articulations of Islamophobia: From the Extreme to the Mainstream?" *Ethnic and Racial Studies Review* 40 (13): 2151-2179.

Nadeem, S., R. B. Horowitz, V. T. Chen, M. W. Hughley, J. Eastman, and K. J. Cramer. 2017. "Viewpoints: Whitewashing the Working Class." *Contexts*, June 23. https://contexts.org/articles/whitewashing-the-working-class/

National Readership Survey. 2008. "National Readership Survey [Online]." Accessed 13 June 2017. http://www.nrs.co.uk/

Neiwert, D., and S. Posner. 2016. "Meet the Horde of Neo-Nazis, Klansmen, and Other Extremist Leaders Endorsing Donald Trump." *Mother Jones*, September 21. http://www.motherjones.com/politics/2016/09/trump-supporters-neo-nazis-white-nationalists-kkk-militias-racism-hate

News, Fox. 2016. "Fox Business". Fox News, March 16. https://www.spiked-online.com/2016/06/30/revolt-of-the-others/

O'Neill, B. 2016. "Brexit Voters are Not Thing, Not Racist: Just Poor." *The Spectator*, July 2. http://www.spectator.co.uk/2016/07/brexit-voters-are-not-thick-not-racist-just-poor/

Patel, J. 2015. ""Both Racism and Anti-Racism Were Present in the Making of the English Working Class": An Interview with Satnam Virdee." *Media Diversified*, November 18. https://mediadiversified.org/2015/11/18/both-racism-and-anti-racism-were-present-in-the-making-of-the-english-working-class/

Peck, T. 2016. "Nigel Farage's Triumphalist Brexit Speech Crossed the Borders of Decency." *The Independent*, June 24. http://www.independent.co.uk/news/uk/politics/brexit-recession-economy-what-happens-nigel-farage-speech-a7099301.html

Phipps, C. 2016. "British Newspapers React to Judges' Brexit Ruling: "Enemies of the People"." *The Guardian*, November 4. https://www.theguardian.com/politics/2016/nov/04/enemies-of-the-people-british-newspapers-react-judges-brexit-ruling

Roediger, D. 1999. *The Wages of Whiteness: Race and the Making of the American Working Class*. New York: Verso.

Rubin, M., N. Denson, K. E. Matthews, T. Stehlik, and D. Zyngier. 2014. ""I Am Working-class": Subjective Self-Definition as a Missing Measure of Social Class and Socioeconomic Status in Higher Education Research." *Educational Researcher* 42 (4):196–200.
Runnymede Trust. 2015. "*The 2015 Budget Effects on Black and Minority Ethnic People.*" Runnymede Trust, http://www.runnymedetrust.org/projects-and-publications/employment-3/budget-2015-impact-on-bme-families.html
Runnymede Trust. 2017. "Race and Class." Runnymede Trust, March 21. http://www.runnymedetrust.org/projects-and-publications/employment-3/race-and-class.html
Rydgren, J. 2013. *Class Politics and the Radical Right*. Abingdon: Routledge. http://libproxy.bath.ac.uk/login?url=http://lib.myilibrary.com?id=423226.
Saini, R. 2017. "Racial Self-Interest' Is Not Racism: Populist Correctness Gone Mad?." *Media Diversified*, March 23. https://mediadiversified.org/2017/03/23/racial-self-interest-is-not-racism-populist-correctness-gone-mad/
Sayer, D. 2017. "White riot—Brexit, Trump, and Post-Factual Politics." *Journal of Historical Sociology* 30 (1): 92–106. doi:10.1111/johs.v30.1.
Song, M. 2014. "Challenging a Culture of Racial Equivalence." *British Journal of Sociology* 65: 107–129. doi:10.1111/1468-4446.12054.
Spiked! 2016. "The Brexit Vote Was a Revolt against the Establishment." *Spiked!/World Bytes*, August 24. http://www.spiked-online.com/newsite/article/the-brexit-vote-was-a-revolt-against-the-establishment/18693#.WWZEVYjytPY
Stewart, H., and R. Mason. 2016. "Nigel Farage's Anti-Migrant Poster Reported to Police." *The Guardian*, June 16. https://www.theguardian.com/politics/2016/jun/16/nigel-farage-defends-ukip-breaking-point-poster-queue-of-migrants
Todd, S. 2015. *The People: The Rise and Fall of the Working Class*. London: John Murray.
Travis, A. 2009, "Denham Takes Aim at White Working-Class Resentment." *The Guardian*, October 14. https://www.theguardian.com/society/2009/oct/14/denham-white-working-class-resentment
Travis, A. 2016. "Lasting Rise in Hate Crime after EU Referendum, Figures Show." *The Guardian*, September 7. https://www.theguardian.com/society/2016/sep/07/hate-surged-after-eu-referendum-police-figures-show
Vance, J. D. 2017. *Hillbilly Elegy: A Memoir of A Family and Culture in Crisis*. London: Harper.
Virdee, S. 2014. *Race, Class and the Racialised Outsider*. Basingstoke: Palgrave.
Virdee, S., and B. McGeever. 2017. "'Racism, Crisis, Brexit'." In *Ethnic and Racial Studies: Race and Crisis* Special Issue, edited by Virdee and Gupta, 1802-1819. 41/10.
Wearing, D. 2017. "Labour Has Slipped Rightwards on Immigration. That Needs to Change". *The Guardian*, July 25. https://www.theguardian.com/commentisfree/2017/jul/25/labour-immigration-jeremy-corbyn-attitudes?CMP=share_btn_tw
Weaver, M. 2016. "'Horrible Spike' in Hate Crime Linked to Brexit Vote, Met Police Say." *The Guardian*, September 28 https://www.theguardian.com/society/2016/sep/28/hate-crime-horrible-spike-brexit-vote-metropolitan-police
Winter, A. 2017. "Brexit and Trump: On Racism, the Far Right and Violence." *Institute for Policy Research (IPR) Blog*, April 3. http://blogs.bath.ac.uk/iprblog/2017/04/03/brexit-and-trump-on-racism-the-far-right-and-violence/
Winter, A. 2018. "The Klan Is History: A Historical Perspective on the Revival of the Far-Right in "Post-Racial" America." In *Historical Perspectives on Organised Crime*

and Terrorism, edited by J. Morrison, A. Silke, J. Windle, and A. Winter, 109–132. Abingdon: Routledge.

Withnall, A. 2016. "Donald Trump Says Nigel Farage Would Make a 'Great' US Ambassador." *The Independent*, November 22. http://www.independent.co.uk/news/world/americas/donald-trump-nigel-farage-us-ambassador-make-great-a7431166.html

Milo Yiannopoulos, B. 2017. "Milo on Why the Democrats Lost the White Working Class." *Breitbart*, January 26. http://www.breitbart.com/milo/2017/01/26/full-text-milo-democrats-lost-white-working-class/

Denmark's blond vision and the fractal logics of a nation in danger

Peter Hervik

ABSTRACT
Recent research has introduced the notion of fractal logic as a way of rethinking racialization and ideas and practices of nationhood. We have claimed elsewhere that racial reasoning instantiates a specific fractal logic called the *nation in danger*, which can be found in circulating images, soundbites, visual signs, metaphors, and narratives created in political communication, news media, and everyday conversations. In these studies, human reasoning is approached as fractals, which implies that the same structure appears self-similarly at different levels. This article examines the *nation in danger* as a basis for aggressive exclusionary reasoning and practices. Two Danish media events from 2016 are looked at: the segregation of swim classes and the new segregation of schools according to 'nationality' and 'ethnicity.' By using fractal logic, the *nation in danger* operates recurrently at different levels and, consequently, constitutes a form of naturalization of the white nationalism that saturates Danish racial reasoning and public debate.

Introduction

In the last two decades, the Nordic countries have witnessed a new populist focus on national, democratic values, common history, ancestry, and descent, which is expressed in 'verbal radicalisms, political symbolism and political marketing' (Betz cited in Mondon 2013, 13). This seemingly new normal on a Euro-American scale is nourished by a division between a national positively-represented, predominantly white in-group and an external, non-white out-group that is negatively depicted along with its domestic collaborators. These collaborators are individuals or groups, who belong to the in-group, but since they show support for refugees and migrants arriving at the border and visible minorities inside the border, they are increasingly regarded as cowards and traitors. Thus, racializing debates about migrants, refugees, minorities, integration, non-Westerners, Muslims, Roma, and so forth, have saturated the public debates as well as policies in a process that involves neo-nationalism, neo-racism, white entitlement, anti-multiculturalism, anti-feminism, anti-cultural Marxism, anti-left, and much more.

In adopting the discourse of neo-nationalism in Denmark, which includes borders, invaders, infiltrators, traitors, cowards, policemen, military personnel, the home guard, and other figures, the Other of this nationalism is, by definition, a racialized foreign other. This Other is variously characterized as 'non-Westerners', 'Muslims', 'parallel society', 'ethnicity', 'terrorists', and 'radicalized'. While the nationalist division is sharp and undeniable in its identity politics that intends to defend and strengthen the 'real', 'authentic', 'true', 'authoritarian', 'Danish' values from unwanted foreign racialized others, on closer inspection, the boundary is a fractal boundary. Seen from a distance, these groups are sharply divided, but as the lens seeks to zoom in on the border, the division is everything but straight and clear; for instance, in identifying who is 'ethnic', 'Muslim', 'Danish', 'non-Westerner' and subject to increasing surveillance and special austerity measures. In fact, as history has shown us, the in-group produces its own out-group out of a projection of itself, a chimeric monster, a 'figment of social imagination' (Smith 1996), the Other as a product of the nationalist Self – an image of Others with their fixed identities, which is rendered between fact and fantasy (Wexler 2004).

When we turn to the study of the racial order of things, colour racism is prioritized, while the application of everything we know as scholars of racism to anti-Muslim racism and Islamophobia is still in its early phases in racism scholarship and state approaches (Meer 2012). Thus, the French government continues to deny Islamophobia as racism, since Muslims in France are both brown, black, and white, which is, of course, precisely what made Kimberlé Crenshaw nearly three decades ago suggest the term *intersectionality* to capture such denials (1991). For scholars of racism, such as Alana Lentin, demands for Muslims to apologize for terrorist attacks, mediated as 'Islamist', means that it builds on the assumption that there is something particular about Muslims and/or Arabs that makes them capable of carrying out such acts as 9/11. 'The association of Arabs and Muslims with threats against our personal security is the lynchpin of Islamophobia' (Lentin 2008, xv).

The overall goal of this article is to argue that praise of Danish popular consciousness and overvaluation of national values embody both a colour racism and anti-Muslim racism and one that works both across borders and inside the border. We argue that neo-nationalism and neo-racism can fruitfully be approached as a fractal logic, referring to 'never-ending patterns' (Online Etymology Dictionary 2017) and self-similarity across scales (Abraham 1993), which we call *nation in danger*. By introducing this notion of fractal logic as a way to approach the new Danish white nationalism, we hope to be able to offer an understanding of how the mechanisms of carrying out physical borders and social boundary control, neo-nationalism and neo-racism work in the predatory search for new spaces to apply this logic. Instead of seeing this expansion and claims-making about new themes and opportunities of contesting the presence of non-white bodies and practices, the *nation in danger* logic is recursively repeated.

In recent research, we introduced the notion of fractal logics as a new way to rethink racialization and ideas and practices of nationhood (Hervik 2018). We claim that racial reasoning instantiates a specific fractal logic of a nation in danger, which can be found in images, soundbites, visual signs, metaphors, and master narratives created in political communication, news media, and everyday conversations. Fractal logic operates recurrently at different levels and, as a consequence, constitutes a form of naturalization of the white Danish neo-nationalism that saturates Danish racial reasoning and public debate. Fractal logic is expanded upon in the section entitled The Nation in Danger as Fractal.

In this article, we extend the previous analysis to look at two recent media events with special attention to the fractal scalarity in the arguments that move from segregated swim classes to the danger of the nation. The material comes from a larger research project [SERR] under a team research effort to understand racialization in Denmark. This sub-project studies extreme speech online from an ethnographic perspective that includes in-depth interviews with commentators from a broad political spectrum of activists. We draw from a pool of 19 interviews and approximately 35 critical social media events (Hervik 2019). Here, we look at two media events. The first is a story about a club's swim classes in Denmark that allows women to swim without men or the gazes of men. The other story is about the segregation of students according to 'ethnicity' in a school with a diminishing number of indigenous Danish students. In the first story, there is fierce opposition to the segregation, while the second story has attracted much nationalist support for segregation.

With the term 'banal nationalism', Michael Billig (1995) showed the presence of everyday 'flagging' of national symbols and routine ways of thinking and talking within well-established nation-states. In a world divided into nation-states, nationalism could not (like racism) be confined to the periphery's extreme revolt against the nation-state order of things or to the last violent stages of groups fighting to become independent nation-states. 'In established nations, it seems "natural" to suppose that nationalism is an over-heated reaction, which typically is the property of others. The assumption enables "us" to forget "our" nationalism'. (Billig 1995, 37). Banal nationalism extends nationalism to the realm of out-of-awareness transcending the political realm and therefore is also routinely ignored in political theory. The major point of Billig's argument is not so much the presence of the banal nationalism, but instead he argues that the presence and reproduction of banal nationalism is necessary for 'hot' nationalism with its passionate and confrontational stance towards migrants and domestic adversaries, who are considered cowards and traitors (Boe and Hervik 2008).

The use of 'neo' in front of nationalism reflects primarily that the nationalism in established states appears under new conditions and circumstances that we could call the post-1989 world without making this year a hard boundary (Gingrich and Banks 2006). Nationalism did occur and was important before 1989, but by the end of the Cold War, new ideas of inner market and outer fortifications of the EU as well as the decline of blue collar jobs and the power of unions, were some of the new circumstances political entrepreneurs could appropriate and capitalize on (Hervik 2011; Kalb and Halmai 2011). Nationalism is still nationalism with its attempt to match cultural, political, and territorial borders and boundaries, but unlike the historical nation-state building for sovereignty and territorial control wrestled from powers occupying nation-states trying to take as much control as possible, the contemporary neo-nationalism is one that uses nationalism as the ideology of the nation-state against minorities in the countries as well as narratives of clash between the West and the non-West. At the same time, the idea of the homogenous nation in control spreads into the state apparatus and into policies.

One of the most salient markers of neo-nationalism is the warning about 'threatening' others who are so different (Fadel, Hervik, and Vestergaard 1999) and so unwilling to adopt 'Danish values' that they threaten to destroy national cultures (Hervik 2011, 134–136). The discourse of cultural threat and pressure on Danish borders, so important for neo-nationalism, was to be met with claims of the strengthening of Danish values and strengthening border control. With these discourses, 'Danes discovered they were white' (Hervik 1999). *White* is used here in the sense of being more aware of themselves as whites. The fuel for the renewed us-them divisions along national and racial lines does not come simply from the presence of brown adoptees, Muslim workers, and families from Turkey, Pakistan, and Algeria, and from African-American jazz players. Instead, this new nationalism comes like the historical one from political elites (see Giddens 1987; Gellner 1983) and the news media, who, particularly in the 1990's, put 'foreigners' on the top of their agenda, not least of which Bosnian and Somali refugees.

It needs to be said that Danish public debate seldom includes the conceptualization of nationalism, racism, or whiteness. Danish politicians, journalists, and political commentators will instead talk about 'Foreigner Policy' (lit. *udlændingepolitik*), 'Alien's Act', (*Integrationslovgivningen*), 'Political Symbolism' (*symbolpolitik*), a 'Restrictive Foreigner Policy' (*stram udlændingepolitik*), which is a dominant claim repeated almost endlessly and rests upon a nationalist foundation. Due to the strong influence of the communication industry, politicians, company leaders, and spokespersons for larger associations will follow expert advice closely. One of these pieces of advice is to avoid associating themselves with negatively-loaded words and events. 'Nationalism' *is not* a preferred word for identifying a political strategy, regardless of whether or not it is your party's policy or the policy of a rival, and best avoided for its negative associations. The idea is not to convey facts so much as presenting yourself and the company in the most favourable light (Hervik 2008, 2011).

Whiteness, neonationalism and the policy of fear

Neo-nationalism uses a cultivation of an external threat and a media coverage of crisis to racialize people claiming they possess incompatible values and cultures whose bodily presence and cultural symbols are undesired. This new resurgent nationalism, Ghassan Hage (2003) called 'paranoid nationalism', which he sees as negatively motivated as opposed to the old historically enthusiastic kind of nationalism. He argues that paranoid nationalism is predominantly a product of a 'decline of hope', i.e. the kind of social hope capitalism as a social system produces, such as 'equated with dreams of upward social mobility, higher purchasing power of commodities and services, etc'. (109, 140). The nation-state responds with aggressive, paranoid neo-nationalism with zero-tolerance towards migrants, refugees, and asylum seekers, but also towards criminals, explanations of crime, unemployed, homeless, welfare recipients and so on (Hage 2003; Hervik 2008). The discourse of threat and danger is a construction people forget is a historical construction. In the Danish case, it emerged in the late 1990s (Hervik 2011). This communication of a threat produces a feeling of fear and a new rhetoric of securitization. For Daniel Bar-Tal, fear leads further on to a state of constant alertness to face dangers; sensitizes society to semiotic cues that signal dangers that start in the everyday but work as slippery slopes; increases solidarity of the in-group; primes members to act on behalf of society to defeat the enemy and defend society and country (2005, 5). In other words, fear creates distrust of and leads to increased ethnocentrism and intolerance towards out-groups (Ibid.).

At the centre of the new self-aware white nationalism, Arjun Appadurai finds the 'anxiety of incompletion' and the 'fear of small numbers', where a single 'coloured' or 'Muslim-looking' body will remind the nation about its incompleteness (2006). 'Anxiety of incompleteness', 'paranoid nationalism', 'decline of hope', and 'being in a state of crisis' trigger moral outrage and create states of alertness that further legitimize securitization and austerity measures, where moral pressure mounts to challenge legal frameworks of rights and protection.

Michel Ignatieff keenly observed that 'The problem with nationalism is not the desire for self-determination itself, but the epistemological illusion that you can be at home, you can be understood, only among people like yourself and that only people like yourself deserve to be in the house' (Ignatieff 1997). Gleaser et al. argue that the implication is 'that people act more trustworthy when they interact with persons of the same nationality and that they act less trustworthy when they interact with persons of a different race or nationality' (Gleaser et al. as cited in Ahlerup and Hansson 2011).

Against an alleged new cultural threat and its implied fear, neonationalists offer national and masculine authority and reassurance – a firm control of immigration, a zero-tolerance policy toward migrant laborers, and a promise to restore familiar forms of identification, particularly around the nation (Gingrich and Banks 2006). The idea of the nation is the imagined cultural homogeneous population of people bonded together by a destiny and the neo-racial idea that living among ones own 'kind' is natural (Barker 1981).

Within the last decade, the categories of 'whiteness' and 'white privilege' that are born in American racism scholarship have been introduced into the Nordic context (see Andreassen and Vitus 2015). Inspired by post-structuralism and post-colonialism, these trans-disciplinary studies have brought much needed attention and criticism to the social, cultural, political, and racial distribution of privilege and power. While 'whiteness' in a North American context is predominantly associated with extreme right-wing politics and practices, the early 1980s, and strongest in the mid 1990s, which Howard Winant described as: 'The incipient crisis of whiteness' (Winant as cited in Gabriel 1998, 2), the application of 'whiteness' to a Nordic context did not pick up until the 2010s, where it is in its early phases.

Whiteness is – like race and ethnicity – a fluid and changing concept with a certain and, at times, causal relationship to privilege (Roediger 2007 [1991]). This implies that the concept has to be seen as relative to the historical context of its emergence. For the situation in Denmark in the late 1990s, there is reason to be careful not to exaggerate the racial dynamic of the construction of whiteness and white privilege as separate from other reasons for the production of intolerance and sustaining racial inequality, namely nationalism, as well as the growth and nature of the middle class and its concern for downward mobility. Both of these also produce marginalization, exclusion, and enemies (Hervik 2011).

From an anthropological perspective that insists on historicizing both phenomenon we study and the analytical categories, Nordic whiteness studies have yet to thoroughly work out the implications and perils of taking whiteness from a North American context to a new one. Thus, for instance, whiteness in the USA is only loosely connected to the nation-state, whereas the enforcement of the nation-state, including the welfare state, is unavoidable in the construction of the Nordic racial order of things.

The history of the Danish nation-state plays a different role than the state does in the U.S. The emerging Danish historic nationalism and nation-building in the 19th century, which had the relationship to Germany and Sweden as two core Others, build mostly on the German romanticist idea of the nation (Hervik 2011). Danes were engaged with their language, their art, and the royal family back then as well as now, which we see in the build-up of cultural canons and Denmark's canon.

The focus on 'Danishness' does not imply that 'white', 'Whiteness', and 'white privilege' are not important; quite the contrary. Instead, these issues are implicated and inseparable to Danishness, but without being, what Omi and Winant found was the case in the U.S., that race is a master narrative of inequality along the lines of inferiority – superiority (2015).

I have argued that the term 'Danishness' rather than 'whiteness' is at the forefront of public debates and everyday conversations. An un-scientific study showed that the political party called the Danish People's Party has more or less taken ownership of the concept of Danishness and Danish values, which shows that unmarked 'nationalism' is the broader key in public discourse. Close to 50% of the voters associate 'Danishness' with the 'Danish People's Party' (rather than other political parties), and not with whiteness (Klingsey 2008). Other parties' spokespersons found this appalling since this is a kind of Danishness that associates with xenophobia and national conservativism. Yet, even if Danishness associates with democracy, free schools, health care, Tivoli, coziness, the Little Mermaid, the royal family, and the flag, that is not to say 'racial whiteness' is not present in a significant role.

Studies of whiteness have attempted to infer the raciality of the Danishness and the extent to which the dominance of the Danish People's Party's nationalism is able to downplay and deflect notions of racism in a Danish context. The party's policies and communication strategies have successfully dominated not only the news media agenda but also made strong inroads into academia. Racialization and racism are fiercely denied (Myong and Danbolt 2019), and with it, the focus on whiteness and white privilege.

An exclusive scholarly focus on 'whiteness' in these approaches to the Danish situation risk failing to capture that the Othering is born out of nationalism, even though whiteness is part of it. Non-white migrants and the 'culturally different' are racialized and inferiorized not as the old-style moral, intellectually inferiority in itself, but as a (narcissistic) means to build nationalism. The discourse, as seen in The Danish People's party examples and in the Danish debate, is saturated with Islam-critical and Islamophobia slurs, discourse, and policies. As Ghassan Hage says: '...whiteness operates as a symbolic field of accumulation where many attributes such as looks, accent, "cosmopolitanism" or "Christianity" can be accumulated and converted into Whiteness' (2003, 232).

Nationalism consists of actions and arguments based on the claim that this community of people should be given certain special rights within the state (Hervik 2011, 31), but this statement does not capture the aggressive, war-based, threat-constructing, authority-offering policies, practices, and utterances, which Denmark bears witness to in recent years. Instead, I will argue that 'the nation in danger' is a better way of capturing this development.

The nation in danger as fractal

The use of fractal theory is fairly new in social science. In the 1970s, mathematician, Benoît Mandelbrot coined the word *fractal* to conceptualise a phenomenon that did not fit conventional, mathematical logic and as such was apprehended as pathological objects or structure. By a simple formula that recursively feeds itself with the outcome, one calculation becoming input in the next and aided by modern computers, Mandelbrot depicted a mathematical set of all numbers into a three-dimensional axis, where each member has its own point. When this is done with a large number of calculations and plotting points, a pattern emerges with a surprising set of attributes.

Fractals refer to 'never-ending patterns' of 'broken' or 'fragmented' patterns (Online Etymology Dictionary 2017). Fractals are irregular, strange, wrinkled, fragmented geometric shapes that are (at least approximately) self-similar across scales (Abraham 1993). In other words, a fractal is a complex figure, punctuated and folded, and when you zoom in on a section, you will find a version that is just as complex as the figure in its entirety. They are found in and part of nature, thus it is not reducible to either language or mathematics. However, Mandelbrot's brilliance is that he found a formula for scaling up and down and sideways, which eventually made it possible to make visual images of the process. Accordingly, fractal patterns mean that large-scale shapes, or logics, are no more complex than small-scale ones. Moreover, these fractals are self-similar across different scales or at the same scale.

Much inspired by anthropologists, Claudia Strauss and Naomi Quinn's work on connectivism or parallel serial processing in the language of computers (1997), I seek a similar use of fractals as they do of neurons. If human learning worked like the links of neural networks, we could, in a parallel fashion, argue that human reasoning, or the discourse produced by human reasoning, works in a similar way as mechanisms of fractal logic. Instead of hard boundaries and ever-new areas of application and quests for unique differences, we may find certain specific fractal logics producing certain patterns of scalarity in nationalist/racialist reasoning. Similar to notions of the habitus (Bourdieu 1977 [1972]) and 'cultural models' and 'figured worlds' (Holland et al. 1998), fractal logics in human reasoning lie beneath language (and gestures), where they are largely out-of-awareness inclinations that orient and 'naturalize' language, thought, and action. People can seldomly articulate these logics, thus, it is the researcher who infers them through language and gestures (Quinn 2005).

We see the fractal as a figuration of the logic that we identify in racial and nationalist reasoning. Fractals are new to social sciences and do not come with a procedure on how to be studied. That is to say, we did not set out to follow a method for studying fractals. Instead, the analysis of the media events and popular reasoning in interviews revealed certain structures that could best be understood as self-similar repetitions. Thus, the fractal conceptualises the way actors' (racialized) interpretation of specific events or stories follows the same structure/logic as a socially shared key narrative. In a previous article, we showed how criticism and counter-criticism of amusement park rides such as 'Cannibal Rides' and 'Hottentot Cauldron' in an amusement park led to a fractal scalarity. The attack was re-represented as an attack not of the specific rides, or names of rides, but on Danish culture through the introduction of non-Danish culture values that represent a hidden 'foreignness'. The initiator of the critique, Jin Vilsgaard, becomes another agent that endangers the nation, and, thus, open to exclusionary personalized attacks for the protection of the nation. Vilsgaard is asked to leave the country, a demand made on the basis of her Facebook photo, that 'reveals' her brown, so-called 'Asian' features. What is at stake is a fractal logic that operates at different levels excluding certain people from the Danish nation. Similarly, a missing handshake by a conservative teacher with Palestinian descent was transformed in public debates and social media into radical Islam in Denmark. In a third example, an argument about a woman's headscarf becomes 'a spearhead of Islamism'. We argued that these examples reveal the meta-narrative, 'A nation-in-danger' and its exclusionary reasoning worked to reinforce the political subjectivity of Danish neo-nationalism (Hervik 2018).

In the following analysis, I will introduce two examples that further argue that this specific fractal logic of the nation in danger, is the basic logic that is repeated infinitely as the scaling moves up or down and on to new spaces. In the process, I will further explain some of the features of this fractal logic.

Danish public swimming pools: (the nation) under threat

On 26 April 2016, the Danish national daily newspaper *Berlingske* published the story, 'New-Danish girls take over the swimming pool – if it is emptied of boys' (*Nydanske piger indtager svømmehallen – hvis den er fri for drenge*) about swim classes for women only in public swimming pools in the capital area of Denmark (Berlingske 2016a). These measures, it appeared from the article, are part of a project aiming at getting more girls with ethnic minority backgrounds to join the leisure centres and learn how to swim. The project started in 2013, and since, have had 246 girls from the age of five to twelve participate, although the swim classes are open to all women. According to the director of the capital's leisure swimming centres, Lars Sørensen, the gender segregation is a new way to reach girls and women who are often absent in swim classes due to religious beliefs. He further states that the project, which also includes the possibility of offering so-called burkinis to girls training in non-segregated teams to become swim coaches, actually strengthens integration. With the present initiative, girls with minority backgrounds come to the swimming pool, where they meet and are taught by role models from their own neighbourhood while they also learn how to swim (Ibid).

By framing the story with a headline about 'New Danish girls' and 'taking-over', the newspaper brings about the idea of a nation in danger. This framing seemed to funnel other newspapers into writing their own version of the story from a similar angle. The daily newspaper, *Politiken*, took the story to national-level politicians, who mostly used moral-panic statements about the practice of segregated swim classes: 'insane', 'retarded', 'absurd', 'grotesque', and 'total failure'. The story about the club also reached the Danish parliament (*Folketinget*), where political leaders and ministers lined up in a row ready to denounce the initiative and criticized it for being 'misunderstood' or 'outright' anti-integration. The girls might very well learn to swim, the argument went, but providing the option of segregated swimming approves patriarchal and hidebound views of women, which is incompatible with Danish society or values (Berlingske 2016b; Politiken 2016).

The comments by sources in the newspapers and by authors in social media exchanges fall in roughly two groups. One set of statements explicitly employs the nation in danger fractal logic and approaches issues involving ethnic minorities as symbols of unwanted presence more generally. The second set of comments are event-near, pragmatic, rational statements that occasionally stray into different but similar activities to segregated swimming, for example, a fractal logic at the same scale but spaced out horizontally. For instance, both bathing and toilets are separated in public schools.

While the case at hand is strictly about a swim club that aims to incorporate women with ethnic minority backgrounds, yet welcomes any woman who wishes to swim without the presence of men or the gaze of men, then the first group of comments collapses the pool itself into 'the nation' in bigoted language about Denmark and what *Danish* is. Examples are statements like: 'are we living in Denmark or in an Islamic caliphate?'; 'Segregated swimming is not Danish'; 'Soon, pig breeding will be prohibited, since certain citizens with a specific religion cannot breathe the same air as pigs'.; 'Those who cannot behave themselves according to Danish norms must be expelled'; and 'Every time we give them an inch they will take a mile'. Commentators re-frame the micro-level swim arrangement and enter a different level of abstraction with statements like: 'This is not Denmark'; 'This is not Saudi Arabia'; and 'The girls come from families, where there isn't a democratic and real gender equality'. These statements are agonistic in the sense that they are not dealing with the original issue at hand, but rather adhere to ritualized discourse building upon an underlying sense of a nation in danger (Tannen 2002, 1652). Letting the girls be segregated is seen as a slippery slope that ends up with a foreign, religious, cultural, inferior take-over of the country.

The second pragmatic set of comments, illustrated with a statement from the head of the swim club and social media commentators, respond more closely to the actual case. Instead of lifting statements into the nation in danger logic, commentators seek to naturalize and neutralize the segregated swim classes by stretching the argument out to similar activities. Some of the statements emphasize the norms already in existence like segregated physical education classes in public schools; segregated toilets for boys and girls; sports-activities separated into girls' teams and boys'; and separate rooms for changing clothes and showering; as well as cooking classes for men only. While different fractal logics may be in place in these arguments, they do not conform directly to the nation in danger logic. Indirectly, they appeal to a logic that is meant to counter the nation in danger fractal, and by doing this they extend the same logic horizontally onto self-similar examples.

The first set of comments rely on a fractal scalarity that works around categorical identities rather than actual persons. Commentators react to the 'segregation' of swim classes as the intention of 'immigrants', that is non-Danes, or outsiders, and their attempt to shape, change, and eventually take over Denmark. The practice is deemed 'incompatible' and stakes are raised by using metaphors for mentally disabled minorities ('insane', 'retarded') onto ordinary women, who prefer to swim in a male-free environment, and thus infusing them with norm-breaking, non-Danish, 'crazy' values. Then, commentators take this further by evoking apartheid, the caliphate, Saudi Arabia, religious fanatics and infuse them with calls for expulsion. The fractal logic is the same, but scaling up seeks to introduce more power into the necessity of protection and securing the nation, or swimming pool, from foreign dangers. In this logic, which we see as vertical, the 'slippery slope' strategy is a fractal scalarity movement. As a result of the debate, which lasted 2–3 days, the word *svømmehal* [public swimming pools] suddenly became part of the anti-immigrant vocabulary – loaded with implicit meaning – as referring to a site in which the battle of Denmark and Danish values is taking place.

This is clear in comments by actors who criticize the initiative, for example, in a commentary thread on the newspaper *Jyllands-Posten*'s Facebook page in 2016. Critics shifted the focus from the minority women's swimming practice onto Denmark and Danish culture and people based on the belief that if you give in to small changes, large transformations will take place, including Islamization and Muslim takeover aided by complicit left-wingers or the ever-so-naïve, Social Liberal party. The basic message is that segregated swim classes are a slippery slope through which Danish culture is being undermined.

Segregation of ethnicities

Four and a half months later, on 6 September 2016, *Morgenavisen Jyllands-Posten*, discussed another story about segregation entitled 'Gymnasium divides students according to ethnicity' (*Gymnasium deler eleverne efter etnicitet*) (Vibjerg and Johansen 2016). The first-year students are divided into four classes exclusively made up of 'immigrants', and three mixed classes 50–50% Danish and non-Danish students. The school has taken this initiative since the number of students with a non-Danish background has gone up to 80% in the most recent first year classes.

The two journalists writing the story, Thomas Vibjerg and Martin Johansen, include sources who comment on the legal aspects of the initiative, while leaving the moral and political commenting to the anticipated follow-up stories. However, they also wrote a separate spin-off story entitled 'This is totally apartheid, right here', supported by a large photograph of five named 'bilingual students'. The story is a feature, where the visible, anonymous (racialized) students are portrayed in the story, as the journalists approach the school.

Within an hour of publishing the internet-version of the story, the national news agency, *Ritzau's Bureau*, brought *Jyllands-Posten's* story, increasing the likelihood of spreadibility from other news outlets. And the story caught on immediately. For example, the national Danish television, Denmark's Radio, and TV2. The next morning, newspapers and television took up the story for themselves and did so in the conventional way of reporting news journalism in the 2000s, namely, asking politicians for comments and letting opposing comments be the actual story. In this process, the scale changed and the legal point of departure in the original story shifted to a moral one.

The first 24 hours of coverage brought a wide spectrum of categorizations of students. The lead article itself used division segregated by 'ethnicity', without specifying what that meant. Students are divided so that 'the ethnic Danish students' are categorized as different from the 'immigrant classes', irrespective of the fact that they are students born in Denmark and therefore technically Danes (they didn't immigrate), which is opposed to the perceived racialized character of the term that operates according to the racial principle 'once ethnic, always ethnic', where 'racial' and 'ethnic' are synonymous. Later, in the same article, the division of students is no longer done along 'ethnic' lines, but last names supposedly to effectively reach 'immigrants' and 'descendants'. Other categorizations in the early coverage are 'total apartheid' (a racial division), 'brown' and 'white' (racial division), 'foreign' classes (national categorization), 'race', 'bilingual' (used as a code word for racial category), 'different cultures' (culture partly replaces race), 'ghetto-schools' (racial category), 'Muslim parallel societies', and 'cultural clash'. It must be emphasized that these categorizations are empirical, or emic, categorization, whereas sociological and anthropological approaches to the categories, most have inferred the nature of us-them, or othering processes, in the categories (Hervik 2011).

The sources used and the comments from social media can again be divided into two roughly divided groups. One group has reservations about the legality of the practice, while the second set of commentators express understanding and acceptance of the school's procedure. The first group is mostly associated with the initial coverage by *Jyllands-Posten*, which brings out the legal framework as the angle of coverage for the practice of dividing students. Spokesperson for Education, for the Liberal Alliance, Merete Risager, is unequivocal: 'You cannot do this. You cannot divide students according to ethnicity in the way it is being done here' (TV2 2016, December 7). The Minister of Education, Ellen Trane Nørby, also makes sure to express what is legal and what is not. 'It goes without saying that you cannot divide students by irrelevant issues (*usaglige forhold*) such as hair colour, skin colour, or ethnicity' (Vibjerg and Johansen 2016). Yet, after Nørby received a report from the school, she concluded that students were divided for pedagogical reasons, which is legal, and not through names, or ethnicity, or race, which is punishable discrimination. She let the school proceed.

The second set of comments express understanding of 'the problem' and use the understanding to express their support of the schools' practice and avoid criticizing the school. Ten days after becoming the new Minister of Education, Merete Riisager, agrees on allowing the school to divide students according to their ethnicity (Ritzau 2016). The Minister of Integration, Inger Støjberg, adheres to the 'fear' that some Danish students have of becoming the minority in their classes: 'I understand well that headmaster, who forms the classes in the gymnasium, so that ethnic Danish students do not become minorities. That has nothing to do with Apartheid' (TV2 2016, September 7). Two 'white Danish' students also appear as sources and fit the second category: "One can best mirror oneself with others, who are a bit like yourself. It is different cultures, and sometimes there are simply some things that fit better with your own culture, which can promote friendships (TV2 2016, September 7). The white nationalist Danes need to be safeguarded from the problem of the 'foreigners', who are annoyingly different. This is the logic in place in most of these comments. When the limit of the number of foreign students has been reached, it is no longer possible to be professional, says professor Niels Egelund (Leonhard and Dohm 2017), and then transforms the debate into one about identity.

The first set of comments are concerned with the legal aspects of racial segregation, or colour-racism legislation. Headlines and comments used loaded racializing terms such as 'ghetto', 'clash', 'apartheid', and 'foreigner'. In this process, the mechanism of fractal scalarity is operating. Students are lumped together under categories of ethnicity and others that ignore their personal histories of being part of Danish society. They are framed and reframed as ethnic, foreigners, and non-Danish, whose presence poses dangers to the indigenous Danes, who are at the threat of becoming a 'minority in our own country'. Such portrayals of oneself as a threatened majority is a method of 'predatory identities' whose social construction and mobilization require the extinction of other, proximate social categories, defined as threats to the very existence of some group, defined as a 'we' (Hervik 2018; Appadurai 2006).

The second set of comments express some reservations, much understanding of the problems with 'non-Danish' students in the classroom. On the basis of Danish students and values being in need of protection, commentators are willing to challenge the legal framework of colour racism. This perspective also relies on a 'foreignization' of students along the lines of Danes and non-Danes.

Conclusion

The whiteness in the Danish racial order of things is an integral part of a neo-nationalist order of things. Studies of whiteness in Denmark have focused mostly on black-white racialization and less on understanding racialization of Islam and Muslims. At the same time, studies of neo-nationalism have struggled with the dialectic use of the 'nation' and the 'West' as units of enlightened celebration. They are different units with different implications but sometimes conflated as the same, and sometimes celebrating the uniqueness of the specific nation next to others.

On closer inspection, the case about segregated swim classes in Copenhagen and the cultural values assigned to the attending women of diverse backgrounds is not a traditional separation of black and white; or, in fact, of men and women. The classes are about women only, with men kept out, while other swim classes are unisex. The separation is that of a few classes of women in the sea of mixed swimming. In the school segregation example, the division is closer to a Jim Crow-type of separation, although it is not directly a separation of whites and blacks, but Danes and non-Danes. Yet, the division of students into exclusionary unisex categories is a national–non-national one. Issues of colour and visibility are obviously strong, since a large portion of the students are non-white and constructed as a problem. In this division, colour racism is a concern of commentators. In the swim class segregation of women from mixed backgrounds, legal aspects were only brought in with regards to who gets to decide. Colour racism issues are not present and Islam-critical and racial Muslim slurs take over.

By introducing the notion of fractal logic, we argue that nation in danger operates recurrently at different levels, and as a consequence, constitutes a form of naturalization of the white nationalism that saturates Danish racial reasoning and public debate. A significant part of the debates around the two media stories, segregation of swim classes, and segregation of students in the gymnasium, is framed around a threat to the nation's borders and internal boundaries that relies on categorization of people in Denmark as non-Danes, or simply foreigners. This foreignness is framed as a danger that may arise at the smallest, seemingly most innocent level, such as offering separate classes for women who feel extra vulnerable with men around, whether in person or their gazes through the windows of the swimming pools, or the everyday experiences in the classroom of too many students of the 'wrong' kind. Threats to the nation and its values calls for protection and pre-emptive initiatives to restore order. When Lisa Malkki argued that the 'national order of things' has become 'the natural order of things', we can argue today that it is also the 'racial order of things', since the fractal logic of the nation in danger builds on a re-framing of identity categories in the local media events into national and racial categories that are.

Disclosure statement

No potential conflict of interest was reported by the author.

Funding

This work was supported by The Study of Experiences and Reactions to Racialization in Denmark under Velux Grant Foundation number 10321.

ORCID

Peter Hervik ⓘ http://orcid.org/0000-0002-5543-7715

References

Abraham, R. H. 1993. "Human Fractals: The Arabesque in Our Mind." *Visual Anthropology Review* 9 (1): 52–55. doi:10.1525/var.1993.9.1.52.

Ahlerup, P., and G. Hansson. 2011. "Nationalism and Government Effectiveness." *Journal of Comparative Economics* 39 (83): 431–451. doi:10.1016/j.jce.2011.05.001.
Andreassen, R., and K. Vitus, eds. 2015. *Affectivity and Race. Studies from the Nordic Context*. Farnham: Ashgate.
Appadurai, A. 2006. *Fear of Small Numbers*. Durham: Duke University Press.
Barker, M. 1981. *The New Racism: Conservatives and the Ideology of the Tribe*. London: Junction Books.
Bar-Tal, D. 2005. "Psychological Obstacles to Peace-Making in the Middle East and Proposals to Overcome Them." *Conflict and Communication Online* 4 (1): 1–5.
Berlingske. 2016a. *Nydanske piger indtager svømmehallen – hvis den er fri for drenge*, April 26.
Berlingske. 2016b. *Støjberg om kønsopdelt svømmetræning: Det kan godt være, vi er nødt til at træffe nogle mere drastiske beslutninger*, April 28.
Billig, M. 1995. *Banal Nationalism*. London: Sage Publications.
Boe, C. S., and P. Hervik. 2008. "Integration through Insult." In *Transnational Media Events. The Mohammed Cartoons and the Imagined Clash of Civilizations*, edited by E. Eide, R. Kunelius, and A. Phillips, 213–234. Gothenburg: Nordicom.
Bourdieu, P. 1977 [1972]. *Outline of a Theory of Practice*. Cambridge: University of Cambridge Press.
Crenshaw, K. W. 1991. "Mapping the Margins: Intersectionality, Identity Politics, and Violence against Women of Color." *Stanford Law Review* 43 (6): 1241–1299. doi:10.2307/1229039.
Fadel, U. H., P. Hervik, and G. Vestergaard. 1999. "De 'besværlige' somaliere." In *Den generende forskellighed*, edited by P. Hervik, 171–213. Copenhagen: Hans Reitzels Forlag.
Gabriel, J. 1998. *Whitewash. Racialized Politics and the Media*. London: Routledge.
Gellner, E. 1983. *Nations and Nationalism*. Oxford: Basil Blackwell.
Giddens, A. 1987. *Social Theory and Modern Sociology*. Cambridge: Polity Press.
Gingrich, A., and M. Banks, eds. 2006. *Neo-Nationalism in Europe and beyond Perspectives from Social Anthropology*. Oxford: Berghahn Books.
Hage, G. 2003. *Against Paranoid Nationalism: Searching for Hope in a Shrinking Society*. Sydney: Pluto Press.
Hervik, P. 1999. *Den Generende Forskellighed. Danske Svar På Den Stigende Multikulturalisme*, Edited by P. Hervik. Copenhagen: Hans Reitzels Forlag.
Hervik, P. 2008. "The Original Spin and Its Side Effects: Freedom Speech as Danish News Management." In *Transnational Media Events. The Mohammed Cartoons and the Imagined Clash of Civilizations*, edited by E. Eide, R. Kunelius, and A. Phillips, 59–80. Gothenburg: Nordicom.
Hervik, P. 2011. *The Annoying Difference. The Emergence of Danish Neonationalism, Neoracism, and Populism in the Post-1989 World*. New York: Berghahn Books.
Hervik, P. 2018. "Re-Figuring the Public, Political and Personal in Current Danish." In *Political Sentiments and Social Movements: The Person in Politics and Culture*, edited by S. Claudia and J. Friedman, 91–117. New York, NY: Palgrave Macmillan.
Hervik, P., ed. 2019. *Racialiation, Racism and anti-Racism in the Nordic Countries*. Series: Approaches to Social Inequality and Difference. New York: Palgrave Macmillan. ISBN 978-3-319-74629-6 (Published August 2018).
Holland, Dorothy, et a ., eds. 1998. *Identity and Agency in Cultural Worlds*. Boston: University of Harvard Press.
Ignatieff, M. 1997. *The Warrior's Honor. Ethnic War and the Modern Conscience*. New York: Holt Paperback, Metropolitan Books/Henry Holt and Company.

Kalb, D., and G. Halmai, eds. 2011. *Headlines of Nation, Subtexts of Class. Working Class Populism and the Return of the Repressed in Neoliberal Europe*. Oxford: Berghahn Books.
Klingsey, M. 2008. "Dansk Folkeparti har erobret Danskheden." *Information*, September 18.
Lentin, A. 2008. *Racism. A Beginner's Guide*. Oxford: A Oneworld Book.
Leonhard, A., and K. Dohm. 2017. "Er grænsen for tosprogede elever nået?" *Jyllands-Posten*, May 18. https://jyllands-posten.dk/premium/indblik/Indland/ECE9589146/er-graensen-for-tosprogede-elever-naaet/
Meer, N. 2012. "Racialization and Religion: Race, Culture and Difference in the Study of Antisemitism and Islamophobia." *Ethnic and Racial Studies* 36 (3): 1–12.
Mondon, A. 2013. *The Mainstreaming of the Extreme Right in France and Australia. A Populist Hegemony?* Farnham: Ashgate.
Myong, L., and M. Danbolt. 2019. "Racial Turns and Returns: Discrediting Danish Research on Racism in Public Media Debates." In *Racialization, Racism and anti-Racism in the Nordic Countries*, 39–61. New York, NY: Palgrave Macmillan.
Omi, M., and H. Winant. 2015. *Racial Formation in the United States*. London: Routledge.
Online Etymology Dictionary. 2017. "'Fractals'. Douglas Harper." http://www.etymonline.com/index.php?allowed_in_frame=0&search=fractal
Politiken. 2016. *Politikere om kønsopdelt svømmehal: 'Grotesk' og 'total fiasko'*, April 27.
Quinn, N., ed. 2005. *Finding Culture in Talk. A Collection of Methods*. New York: Palgrave Macmillan.
Ritzau. 2016. "Langkaer gymnasium får lov at opdele elever efter etnicitet." *Kristeligt Dagblad*, December 8.
Roediger, D. R. 2007 [1991]. *The Wages of Whiteness: Race and the Making of the American Working Class*. New York: Vrso. Revised Edition.
Smith, D. N. 1996. "The Social Construction of Enemies: Jews and the Representation of Evil." *Sociological Theory* 14 (3): 203–240. doi:10.2307/3045387.
Strauss, C., and N. Quinn. 1997. *A Cognitive Theory of Cultural Meaning*, Edited by C. Strauss and N. Quinn. Cambridge: Cambridge University Press.
Tannen, D. 2002. "Agonism in Academic Discourse." *Journal of Pragmatics* 34: 1651–1669. doi:10.1016/S0378-2166(02)00079-6.
TV2. 2016. *Mie og Michelle bakker op: Derfor er det en god løsning at opdele eleverne*, September 7. http://nyheder.tv2.dk/samfund/2016-09-07-mie-og-michelle-bakker-op-derfor-er-det-en-god-loesning-at-opdele-eleverne(09032017)
Vibjerg, T., and M. Johansen. 2016. "Gymnasium deler eleverne efter etnicitet." *Jyllands-Posten*, September 6, Indland Section. Accessed 11 March 2018. https://jyllands-posten.dk/indland/ECE8981416/gymnasium-deler-eleverne-efter-etnicitet
Wexler, J. 2004. "Alterity." *Theories of Media, Keywords Glossary*. University of Chicago.

Are French people white?: Towards an understanding of whiteness in Republican France

Jean Beaman

ABSTRACT
Based on ethnographic research of France's North African second-generation, I bring together literatures on racial formation, whiteness, and race and racism in Europe to discuss how whiteness operates in French society. I discuss how respondents must navigate a supposedly colorblind society in which whiteness is default. Because these individuals are racialized as non-white, they are not seen as French by others. I discuss how they wrestle with definitions of French identity as white and full belonging in French society as centered on whiteness. I argue that salience of whiteness is part of France's racial project in which differences among individuals are marked without explicit state-sanctioned racial and ethnic categories. This has implications for considering how whiteness is crucial to understanding European identity more broadly, including through the rise of the Far-Right, the recent Brexit and Leave campaigns, and anti-immigration sentiment throughout Western Europe.

> France views and portrays itself as a white country. My whole life, I've felt erased by the national narrative. People even keep complimenting me on how good my French is. It's deeply embedded in the national consciousness that [the] 'true' identity is one which has been here forever.
> - Rokhaya Diallo, French journalist and writer of Senegalese origin

In late July 2017, MWASI, a French Afro-feminist collective formed in 2014, held the Nyanspo festival in Paris with the slogan 'Don't Agonize, Organize!' Such a three day festival might otherwise been unremarkable except for the fact that about 80 percent of the festival's schedule was specified for either Black women, women of color, or Black individuals more generally ('espace non mixte femmes noires,' 'espace non mixte femmes racisées,' 'espace non mixte personnes noires') in order for such individuals to reflect on experiences of racism and devise afrofeminist political strategies.[1] As French

Republican ideology dictates that the only meaningful identity is a French one, the festival's 'non-mixte' scheduling immediately drew controversy. It was deemed an 'anti-white' event, one that was racist towards whites. It was accused of being 'communitariste,' the dreaded term in French for separate (ethnic) identity-based communities. Anne Hidalgo, the mayor of Paris, demanded that the festival be cancelled and argued that it violated anti-discrimination laws.[2] La Ligue internationale contre le racisme et l'antisémitisme (The International League against Racism and Anti-Semitism, or LICRA) and S.O.S. Racisme – two French anti-discrimination and anti-racist organizations – also denounced the festival. On Twitter, LICRA declared that 'Rosa Parks must be turning over in her grave.'[3]

In June 2018, Paris's Ecole des Hautes Etudes en Sciences Sociales (The School of Advanced Studies in the Social Sciences) held a day-long symposium on the 'White Condition: Reflections on a French Majority' ('La condition blanche: Réflexion sur une majorité française').[4] Led by social scientists Sarah Mazouz and Mathilde Cohen, the symposium explored the variant ways that whiteness is the standard in French society and how non-white minorities are simultaneously visible and invisible. Yet this conference – the first of its kind in French academia – was also not without its controversy. It was also labelled as racist and anti-white.

Both of these controversies were revealing of how the terms 'white' and 'whiteness' have meaning in French society, despite France's disavowal of such racial and ethnic labels. What is complex about considering what whiteness and white mean in French society is how racial and ethnic terms have no official legitimacy. France does not collect official statistics on race and ethnicity and does not have state-level racial and ethnic categories. There is no category on the French census for white or black. Under the French Republican model, being French is supposed to trump all other identifications and differences such as race and ethnicity are not officially acknowledged.

Yet, there are many ways that race and ethnicity are marked without official designations by the state (Beaman 2017; Keaton 2010; Ndiaye 2008). In what follows, I bring together literatures on whiteness, racial formation, and race and racism in Europe to argue for and demonstrate the salience of whiteness in French society. Specifically, based on ethnographic research in the Parisian metropolitan area, I discuss how middle-class children of North African, or Maghrebin, immigrants in France conceptualize whiteness as default in French society and how they are racialized as non-white.

I further discuss how their racialization as non-white is one indicator of France's ongoing racial project (Omi and Winant 1994) in which the links between whiteness and belonging to France are continually produced and reproduced. Part of this racial project which marks differences among France's populations involves the social construction of whiteness as the default or the norm. I use the example of the middle-class North African second-generation to illustrate how French identity is understood at macro and micro levels as white.

I will first discuss the background to and methodology of this study. I then discuss how whiteness fits into France's racial project and reflects the larger connection between whiteness and Europeanness and European identities as white. In doing so, I connect and apply existing research on racial formation in the United States, whiteness as a social construction, and race and racism in Europe to France in order to demonstrate how French is constructed as white. I then discuss the experiences of middle-class children of North African immigrants in which their exclusion because of their racial and ethnic status was continually reinforced and how they make sense of the construction of French identity as white. I conclude by discussing the implications of the centrality of whiteness in France for other plural societies.

Background

In order to unpack how whiteness is understood by non-white individuals in France, I first discuss the broader context of North African, or Maghrebin, immigrants and their descendants in France.

France's colonial empire in the Maghreb began in Algeria in 1830, in Tunisia in 1881, and in Morocco in 1912. Algeria would remain in French control until 1962 and Tunisia and Morocco would remain in French control until 1956. Though emigration from the Maghreb to France began as early as the early 1900s, World War I brought immigrants from these French colonies *en masse* to France for work. These immigrants, who were expected to only be temporary residents, often settled in the outlying *banlieues*, or suburbs, of major cities because of the presence of cheaper housing and factory employment. The number of Maghrébin immigrants continued to increase with World War II, the end of France's Fourth Republic in 1958, and the Algerian War of Independence in 1962. This increase saw more and more North African immigrants living in subsidized housing complexes (or *habitations à loyer modéré* or HLMs) in the *banlieues*. These Maghrébin immigrants often had low levels of educational attainment than native French and worked in low-skilled employment. Due to an economic recession and declining employment opportunities, France temporarily suspended immigration of non-European workers in 1974. However, this led to migrant workers settling permanently with their families in France as opposed to returning to their home countries (Silberman, Alba, and Fournier 2007). According to the Institut National de la Statistique et des Etudes Economiques (National Institute of Statistics and Economic Studies, or INSEE), which conducts the French census, more than half of the immigrants who arrived before 1974 came for employment-related reasons; and another one third came to join their husbands or family. The North African second-generation – including my respondents – descended primarily from this population (Silberman, Alba, and Fournier 2007). While citizenship status has historically been complicated for children of immigrants (at least partially due to the distinction between citizenship and nationality), currently individuals born in France to Maghrébin immigrants become citizens at 18 years old and are seen to have 'virtual citizenship at birth' (Simon 2012).

Because the French census does not demarcate racial and ethnic origin of citizens due to French Republican ideology, there is a dearth of data on second-generation populations. The available data from the 1999 *Étude de l'histoire familiale* (Study of Family History, or EHF) combines individual country of birth with parent country of birth (see Meurs, Pailhé, and Simon 2006; Tribalat 2004). As of 1999, about 26 percent of second-generation immigrants in France are of Maghrébin origin. Specifically, about 14 percent are of Algerian origin, 9 percent are of Moroccan origin, and 4 percent are of Tunisian origin (Tribalat 2004). The largest survey of the second-generation, the 2009 joint Institut National d'etudes demographiques (National Institute of Demographic Studies, or INED) and INSEE, *Trajectoires et origins*, reports unequal treatment and discrimination towards and a lack of inclusion of second-generation North African immigrants (Simon 2012). This survey also reports that many individuals do not feel accepted as French by others because they are not seen to 'look French' (Simon 2012). Other research on these children of immigrants focuses on their inherited disadvantage from their immigrant parents as well as their disadvantage relative to whites (Lombardo and Pujol 2011; Silberman 2011; Simon 2012). Yet, as of 2003, about 15 percent of second-generation North African immigrant men and about 23 percent of second-generation North African immigrant women hold salaried jobs (Lombardo and Pujol 2011). This is the segment of the Maghrebin second-generation I discuss in this paper.

Data and methodology

Data comes from ethnographic research including semi-structured interviews with 45 middle-class adult children of Maghrebin immigrants living in the Parisian metropolitan region. They were all born and raised in France. The original aim of this study was to understand the experiences of ethnic minorities in France. I focus on middle-class individuals, those who have achieved upward mobility vis-à-vis their immigrant parents. I delineate middle-class by respondents' educational attainment levels and professional statuses. In terms of education, I focus on those who passed the *Baccalauréat* (BAC) exam and attended college (whether or not they actually graduated). In terms of employment, I focus on those in the French socio-professional category of *cadre*. Snowball sampling was used to draw a respondent sample. My respondent sample includes 24 men and 21 women. Respondents range in age from 24 to 49 years old; the average age being 32 years old. In terms of North African origin, about 55 percent are of Algerian origin; about 26 percent are of Moroccan origin; and 17 percent are of Tunisian origin. About 35 percent of respondents live in Paris proper and about 65 percent live in the *banlieues*, namely the inner-ring *départements* of Seine-Saint-Denis, Val-de-Marne, and Hauts-de-Seine. All interviews were recorded and later transcribed. Interview transcripts were then coded using a grounded theory approach (Strauss and Corbin 1990) for emergent themes related to whiteness and the nature of French identity. All respondents' names are pseudonyms per Institutional Review Board guidelines.

Race, racism, and whiteness in Europe

My thinking about the significance of whiteness in France is informed by how race and racism operates in Europe more generally, particularly in contexts where racial categories are not explicitly acknowledged or measured. David Theo Goldberg's (2006) framework of racial Europeanization is instructive here for how race and racism are framed throughout Europe – either as exceptional, i.e. as pertains to the Far Right, or as phenomena of the past, i.e. as in the Holocaust. To Goldberg, race is often framed very narrowly, yet orders and makes the nation-state throughout Europe, even without explicit categories. Europe therefore is silent about race, despite ample evidence of its significance in everyday life across the continent (Lentin 2008).

Part of Europe's silence about race and racism is also a silence about whiteness. Goldberg further argues that being seen as European, or a part of Europe, is predicated on being white:

> The taboo of racial characterization, and the at least official avoidance of racial expression or categorization, reinforce the long historical presumption of Europe as the home of whiteness and Christianity. It follows that any person of color or non-Christian (at least genealogically) in Europe presumptively is not of Europe, not European, doesn't (properly or fully) ever belong. Just as, historically, anyone whose ancestry was considered to emanate from elsewhere was deemed non-European (Goldberg 2009, 179–180).[5]

Goldberg further argues that Islamophobia and xenophobia in Europe is fueled by a fear of Europe becoming non-white, or the encroachment of non-white individuals into Europe:

Europe's racial self-articulation has long expressed itself in terms of the denial, exclusion, and ultimately the purging of those not white – not European, to be emptily, circularly precise – from first its ideational conception and then also from what it has taken as its territory (Goldberg 2009, 187).

These are the processes for maintaining Europe for particular Europeans, not unlike the desire to the maintain France for particular French individuals, as articulated by the Front National, France's Far Right political party. Despite years of colonialism and related immigration, non-white individuals are continually seen as non-European. To the extent that immigrants were or are acknowledged, it was as temporary residents, not potential members of the nation-state. As all racial and ethnic categories are social constructions, whiteness is also a social construction, which in Europe is based upon colonial domination of other countries.

Much extant empirical research links whiteness and national identities throughout Europe, albeit not often focused on France. Europeanness is framed similar to whiteness, particularly in terms of societal power relations (Kaufmann 2006; Keskinen 2017; Weiner 2012). That white is synonymous with national identities often exists in contexts that purport to be colorblind or otherwise race-blind (Moschel 2011). Whiteness is at the core of various national identities. For example, Keskinen (2017) demonstrates how whiteness is at the core of national identities in Nordic countries which also serves to ignore or deny racial histories. In the context of the United Kingdom, British as white is a default category into which it is impossible for other individuals to integrate. To Byrne's (2007) white women interviewees living in London, being English is defined as being refined, middle-class, and above all, white. Central to this discussion is the fear of losing English identity or the fear of England becoming less English due to an influx of immigrants, among other phenomena. Cretton (forthcoming) demonstrates how Switzerland has a racial logic in which race is not acknowledged, yet non-white individuals are assumed to be non-Swiss. Being white and being Swiss are seen as synonymous, and black comes to stand in for characteristics seen as incompatible with Swiss national and cultural identity. Similarly, in Germany, who is and who is not German is a distinction often based on race and ethnicity, in which an individual who is not white is seen as suspect as German (Müller 2011). In the Netherlands, the Dutch terms 'autochthon' (from this soil) and 'allochthon' (from another soil) function as ethnic and racial labels for Dutch and non-Dutch individuals (Essed and Trienekens 2008). Moreover, the hidden curriculum in Dutch schools serves to promote values associated with being white in the Netherlands, despite the actual ethnic diversity in the Netherlands (Weiner 2015). In Norway, the term 'white' is often reserved for individuals who are thought to be culturally similar enough to assimilate to mainstream society-or individuals closest to Norwegian. In common parlance, schools are described as black schools when a large percentage of the students are immigrants, regardless of their origin or skin pigmentation (Alba and Foner 2015).[6]

Whiteness and France's racial project

In considering what whiteness means in the French context, I apply two theoretical frameworks developed outside of France, namely whiteness studies and racial formation. First, I discuss the salience of race and racism in France. Despite the Republican denial of the significance of race and ethnicity, several scholars of French history (Kastoryano 2004; Peabody and Stoval 2003; Wieviorka 1992) have argued that France has long relied on racial and ethnic boundaries in constructing its national identity, particularly in terms of what occurred outside of the 'Hexagon,' namely colonial rule and slavery. Furthermore, other scholars have noted how French Republicanism has been used to minimize both the long history of international migration to France, including from its former colonies, and the multicultural nature of French society (Chabal 2015; Noiriel 1996). Moreover, despite the repeated disavowal of race in France, many have demonstrated how racism, as well as race, are salient in French society across micro, meso, and macro levels (Fanon 1967; Kastoryano 2004; Keaton 2010; Jugé and Perez 2006; Simon 2012).

The significance of race and racism despite the official denial of both also relates to notions of who can and who cannot be included in France. For example, in 1967's *Black Skin, White Masks*, Frantz Fanon, the Martinique-born writer and philosopher quickly understood that he could never be seen as French despite having been born in the French *département* of Martinique and spent time in the French hexagon. He writes of how 'white civilization and European culture have forced an existential deviation on the Negro' (1967, 14). Therefore blacks in France are not seen as of France. Fanon demonstrates how colonialism and slavery have created the boundaries of inclusion and exclusion in the construction of France. This is another way of considering how whiteness and blackness are co-constitutive of each other, and how whiteness as synonymous with Frenchness relies on being black as the opposite of being French. His work suggests that discourses established through colonialism continue to benefit whiteness. Even though *race* as a term exists in the French language, the National Assembly suppressed its use in legislation in 2013 (Beydoun 2013). It is this context that makes race in France both necessary and difficult to discuss. I argue that France is undergoing a racial project, per Omi and Winant (1994) formulation. In such a racial project, 'racial categories are created, inhabited, transformed, and destroyed' (Omi and Winant 1994, 55). It is a way of making meaning out of differences, which are historically and socially informed, among individuals. In France, a racial common sense is created in a seemingly colorblind society.[7]

Racial meaning is applied without officially substantiating racial and ethnic categories, so that the North African second-generation – as well as other ethnic minorities – can be racialized in a context in which the only meaningful identity is a French one. Other scholars have demonstrated how Maghrébin-origin individuals and other ethnic minorities are racialized as non-white or 'other' (Beauchemin et al. 2010; Kastoryano and Escafré-Dublet 2012; Keaton 2009, 2010; Simon 2012; Silverstein 2008). In this context, race 'signifies and symbolizes social conflicts and interests by referring to different types of human bodies' (Omi and Winant 1994, 55), which 'form a distinctive stigmata of inferiority' (Keaton 2010, 106).

Just as French Republicanism denies the existence of race and racism, I argue that it simultaneously denies the existence of whiteness and white supremacy. Part of France's racial project is the continued production and reproduction of white as normal or default. Such production dates from the construction of the nation itself; French culture is portrayed as an unchanging, homogenous entity (Beaman 2017). As the two examples I discussed at the beginning of this paper suggest, white supremacy is often mobilized as anti-white racism (Fleming 2017). In fact, Gallagher and Twine argue that whiteness itself is a racial project, in that 'it only derives its political meaning in relation to other groups within a racial hierarchy' (2017, 1599).

As I discussed in the last section regarding how whiteness functions in Europe more broadly, whiteness becomes synonymous with national identity in a context in which whiteness is synonymous with citizenship and full societal belonging. Garner (2016) delineates four frames of how whiteness is constructed and racialized within the United Kingdom, including how whites see themselves as victims and how individuals cannot define who is British but could easily define who is not British. From the conception of the United States, American citizenship was originally only available to 'free white men'. As such, whiteness was and is both legally and socially constructed as there was a direct connection between being legally determined to be white and being a citizen (Harris 1993). This is another way of considering how whiteness is normalized, commonplace, or as Bonilla-Silva (2012) refers to is, part of 'racial grammar'. Such 'racial grammar' serves to embed our discourse with whiteness, normalize whiteness, and preserve the way of things, including the domination of individuals categorized as white (Twine and Gallagher 2008). Part of the examination of whiteness is making visible both white supremacy as well as whiteness in terms of power relations (Emirbayer and Desmond 2015; Garner 2017). Both Hughey (2010) and Lewis (2004) refer to whiteness as 'hegemonic' in American society, which allows us to consider the shared meanings of whiteness by Americans racialized as white. Specifically, it refers to 'a shifting configuration of practices and meanings that occupy the empty space of "normality" in our culture. Collectively, this set of schemas functions as that seemingly "neutral" or "precultural" yardstick against which cultural behaviour, norms, and values are measured' (Lewis 2004, 634).

While there has been focus on whiteness in other parts of Europe, less has been written on how whiteness structures France. This is perhaps because of how the French Republican model makes it difficult to see French as a racialized category and in turn, makes whiteness to tease out. Moreover, the Republican ideology enables a colorblind logic in which racism is not explicated mentioned and it is seen as racist to invoke race. Unpacking France's racial project requires discussing whiteness because the racialization of Maghrébin-origin individuals and other racial and ethnic minorities exists in a context in which whiteness is the standard. In what follows, I discuss how non-white individuals – here, Maghrebin-origin individuals – understand how whiteness operates in French society.

French as white to non-whites

'Many people think being French, it's being white, eating pork, going to mass every Sunday morning, being Catholic and so on … But me, I say being French is not that, for me being French is simply working in this country, paying taxes, it's just living here'. So explained Nasser, a 36 year old of Algerian origin who was born and raised in Seine-Saint Denis, a *département* north of Paris. As we sat in his office at the television station where he has worked as a journalist for a number of years, surrounded by cubicles and television monitors, he explained his difficulties being the only non-white person where he works. This is in contrast to his *banlieue* community where most residents are immigrant-origin individuals – or as Nasser puts it, '*les issus de la colonialisation,*' or descendants of France's colonial empire in North and Sub-Saharan Africa.

One another occasion when we were taking the tram to his apartment, he pointed out all the North African and Sub-Saharan origin individuals on the tram and on the streets as we rode by. 'How could you feel French in a community like this?,' he asked rhetorically. Nasser challenges the racial and ethnic nature of what it means to be French, yet also recognizes that French people see being white as a prerequisite for being French or being included in French society. He acknowledges how others see being French as synonymous with being white affects him. Even though he sees himself as part of France–however complicated that is for him–because he is not white, he is not seen by others as part of France.

Moreover, the French term, *français de souche*, which technically means native-born French individuals is never used for second or subsequent generation immigrant populations. In other words, native-born French individuals are understood to be white. Individuals like Nasser are usually referred to as foreigners or immigrants, even though as people born and raised in France, they are neither.[8]

In a September 2015 interview with France 2 Television, Nadine Morano, a *Les Républicains* party politician, stated the following: 'In order to have a national cohesion, it is necessary to keep equilibrium, meaning the cultural majority. We are a Judeo-Christian country – as General de Gaulle said – of the white race, which attracts foreigners. I want France to remain France. I don't want France to become Muslim.' *Les Républicains* is a center-right political party formed in 2015, when former president Nicolas Sarkozy renamed the *Union pour un mouvement populaire* (UMP). Morano's comments convey not only how Muslim is a racialized category located at the bottom of France's racial and ethnic hierarchy, but also how it is in opposition to whiteness and the idea of a 'true France.' Despite French Republicanism which negates race and ethnicity as actual categories, French itself is a racialized identity.

The North African second-generation is one population that is racialized, which occurs simultaneously with the construction of French as white and France as a white nation. As has been demonstrated elsewhere (Beaman 2017), despite many children of Maghrebin immigrants feeling French as part of their own identities, they are still kept on the margins of French society and are perceived by fellow French individuals as not French. According to French demographer Patrick Simon, 'This dissonance is undeniably a source of tension and generates feelings of rejection. While the French population is ethnically and religiously diverse, this diversity is not yet fully incorporated in the representation of Frenchness' (2012, 13). They are 'visible minorities' (Ndiaye 2008) because they are not white, and it is this visibility that excludes them from fully belonging in France.

Karim, a 32-year-old of Algerian origin who lives in Malakoff, a *banlieue* south of Paris, is one example of this phenomenon, as well as of the upwardly-mobile segment of the Maghrébin second-generation. Despite his parents not being attending school past the age of 14 and working in only menial kinds of employment, Karim is well-educated and an accomplished journalist. Yet this upward mobility does not minimize the racism he and others experience. 'People still see being French as being white,' he explained. 'Everything is fine so long as Maghrebin individuals are relegated to being gangsters or criminals, but once they become doctors, like my wife, then more and more people feel threatened. And people are even more racist.' In other words, the increased visibility of Maghrebin-origin individuals like himself and his wife in middle-class positions in society challenges conceptions of French society as white. Such a perceived 'threat' only heightens the exclusion this population faces. Moreover, Karim and others live in a French Republican society that not only disavows race and ethnicity as bases for identity but also communities based on identities.

But Karim believes this is only true for racial and ethnic minorities in France. 'Whites can just be individuals, they are just French. A group of whites is not seen as a group or a community but whenever there is a group of blacks or Maghrébins, they are accused of being communitarianist,' he explained. Whiteness is the default in French society (Ndiaye 2008). As such, the connection between French and white operates at both individual and institutional levels (Jugé and Perez 2006). Therefore, there is nothing exceptional about whites congregating amongst themselves, yet it becomes visible and problematic when people of color do it. Karim further clarified for me how many Maghrebin-origin and sub-Saharan African-origin individuals live far from the center of Paris–often in neighborhoods with poor transportation to the city and few employment opportunities. 'But they did not choose to live in those neighborhoods, they were put there,' he explained. Karim thinks these conditions in France are only getting worse. He hears the word 'white' more today than when he was growing up, as if people are more explicit in discussing who belongs and who does not in France.

As I have argued elsewhere (Beaman 2015), many middle-class children of Maghrebin immigrants refer to the legal dimensions of being French over its cultural dimensions in order to assert themselves as French. As does Nasser, they acknowledge that many people see being French as being synonymous with being white, yet they challenge this conception by defining being as French as having legal ties to the nation. So even if they are excluded from the cultural dimensions of being French or from actually being included in French society, they can still assert that they are technically French because they are French citizens. Noura, a 30 year old of Algerian origin who lives in Drancy, a northeastern *banlieue* of Paris, similarly asserts a place for herself and other children of North African immigrants in French society, while also recognizing its various inherent problems:

> We have to combat this myth that to be French means you have to be white, or you have to have Judeo-Christian background ... there should be no hierarchy between children who come from a long line of French relatives and children of immigrants ... Minorities are often not seen as legitimate. The media only focuses on their problems, not their successes.

Even though technically Noura and other children of North African immigrants have a claim to being a part of French society, they acknowledge that they are not treated as such. Being French is often not equated with having French citizenship but involving 'cultural markers of birth, ancestry, and accent as well as residence' (McCrone and Bechhofer 2010, 921). And these cultural markers are sustained by racial and ethnic distinctions. The boundaries around French identity require whiteness and the exclusion of immigrant-origin individuals tied to its colonial empire, which is why the North African second-generation can never fully belong despite their assertions to the contrary. France therefore continues to perpetuate racism and white supremacy despite its colorblind racial ideology.[9]

One way that difference is marked in France outside of explicit racial and ethnic categorization is through language related to immigration, as I discussed earlier. The Maghrébin second-generation is often described as foreigners or in related to the immigration of their parents, rather than their native-born existence in France. But this is different for 'white' children of immigrants in France. For example, former French president Nicolas Sarkozy is a second-generation French person, as he was born in France to a Hungarian immigrant father. Yet his immigrant origin posed no barrier to his political career or ascension to the French presidency. He was and is seen as French and was never considered not French. I argue that this because Sarkozy is white, and therefore it was not difficult to imagine him as representative of French society. Such success is almost unimaginable for an individual of Algerian, Moroccan, or Tunisian origin. He or she would not be considered a legitimate member of the French Republic. Sabri, a 30 year old of Tunisian origin, recalled how Sarkozy once likened himself to Obama in an interview, on the grounds that both were children of immigrants, though Sabri noted that 'the son of a white immigrant is not the son of a black immigrant. It's not the same thing.'

The differentiation between Sarkozy and Maghrebin and other non-white descendants of immigrants is further illustrative of how non-whites are only provisional guests in French society. Goldberg (2006) notes this as well, writing, "The idea of the European excludes those categorically as non-European, as being not white. [It says] You are here but don't (really or fully) belong. Your sojourn is temporary, so don't get too comfortable' (347). Many respondents are continually asked where they are from, as if France could not conceivably be an answer to that question.

Discussion: whiteness in France and beyond

Here, I have brought together literatures on whiteness, race and racism, and racial formation and applied them to the French context to illustrate how non-white individuals conceptualize French identity as a white one. I have used the example of the middle-class segment of the Maghrebin second-generation in order to unpack France's racial project and demonstrate how whiteness as the norm is part of this racial project. Even though many respondents see being French as constitutive of their identities, they understand that their compatriots do not see them as French which they attribute to their being non-white. The racialization of French identity as white exposes the tensions of French Republicanism, which both directly and indirectly denies France's longstanding ethnic diversity due to its colonial and immigration histories. Considering how whiteness operates in France through the perspectives of non-white individuals also illustrates how white and whiteness can have social meaning, even in a society where they do not 'exist' and purports to be colorblind.

France is a society often obsessed with losing its identity. The Front National has capitalized on this 'crisis' through an 'Islamization of France' rhetoric, or the idea that French identity is being eroded by the growing presence of Muslims, or non-whites more generally. This partly explains why, for example, having Halal food at supermarkets or removing pork from school cafeteria menus generates so much controversy (Almeida 2017). I argue that this also relates to how whiteness is continually in crisis, and how it continually reinforces itself in response to this crisis. As such, protecting French identity requires protecting whiteness as default. My thinking of how white identity or whiteness is seen as a default in French society relies upon a broader construction of European identity or Europeanness as white. As white supremacy is global (Weiner 2012), considering how it operates in France reveals how France is also a part of a global racial and ethnic hierarchy.

Moreover, I am reminded of Stuart Hall's example of tea as a symbol of the United Kingdom – another context where whiteness is the default category. Yet tea is a product of the British colonial empire in India, as 'not a single tea plantation exists within the United Kingdom' (1991, 49). This image of a homogenous white society contradicts the non-white component of the U.K. And more recently, whiteness as default relates to recent immigration-related events in Europe. The case of Brexit in the U.K., the vote for the U.K. to leave the European Union, can largely be understood through xenophobic and racist sentiment and a fear of losing an essential British cultural identity. Similarly, the rise of the Far Right in societies besides France, such as Germany or the Netherlands, and the so-termed Syrian refugee crisis and how different European societies have responded to it reflect how whiteness is central to discussions who is an ideal citizen or ideal member of society (Garner 2017).

In titling this article with the question as to whether or not French people are white, I sought to interrogate how understandings of French identity are racialized and synonymous with whiteness, as well as how people outside of those definitions understand the relationship between whiteness and French identity. Yet, as Fanon aptly illustrated, blackness and whiteness are co-constitutive of each other, therefore a focus on the racial and ethnic othered populations must include a consideration of how whiteness sustains such otherness. Therefore, if Fanon was understood as Black and not French, being French is understood as white.

Notes

1. https://nyansapofest.org/.
2. https://www.lemonde.fr/societe/article/2017/05/28/anne-hidalgo-demande-l-annulation-d-un-festival-en-partie-interdit-aux-blancs_5135073_3224.html; https://www.washingtonpost.com/news/global-opinions/wp/2017/06/12/why-its-so-hard-for-minorities-in-france-to-find-safe-spaces/?utm_term=.2ce93a581320 I should note that a compromise was reached in terms of the festival in which the exclusive events would be held at the private venues and the festival events that were open to everyone could be held at private venues.
3. https://twitter.com/_LICRA_/status/868123586518757376?ref_src = twsrc%5Etfw%7Ctwcamp%5Etweetembed%7Ctwterm%5E868123586518757376%7Ctwgr%5E373939313b636f6e74726f6c&ref_url = https%3A%2F%2Fwww.lemonde.fr%2Fsociete%2Farticle%2F2017%2F05%2F28%2Fanne-hidalgo-demande-l-annulation-d-un-festival-en-partie-interdit-aux-blancs_5135073_3224.html.
4. https://global-race.site.ined.fr/fr/evenements/autres-manifestations/.
5. Part of this is due to the conflation between European and Christian as identities (Bonnett 1998).
6. Moreover, this is similar to equating whiteness with 'eliteness.' Ayling (2017) argues that the colonial relationship between Nigeria and the UK has colored Nigerian parents' perceptions of quality education which leads them to prefer sending their children to private schools in the UK, versus high-quality schools in Nigeria.
7. Although Omi and Winant (1994) theoretical frameworks of racial formation and the racial project have been criticized as solely applicable to the United States, I suggest that their frameworks are quite applicable to non-United States contexts as, among other characteristics, they do not rely on Black/White binaries. In addition, I would like to challenge the idea that an American understanding of race and ethnicity is completely divorced from a European one, particularly when considering the interlinking histories of slavery by both the United States and several European countries (Goldberg 2006).
8. This is not unlike the experiences of people of color in other plural societies, including the United States, where they have to contend with whiteness as the default for national identities (see Trieu and Lee 2016).
9. One example of this is how so-called neutral laws have disparate outcomes based on race and ethnicity (Moschel 2011).

Acknowledgments

I thank Nasar Meer for organizing this special issue and for his feedback and guidance. I also thank the reviewers for their useful comments and suggestions. Finally, I thank respondents for their generosity and participation. All errors are my own.

Disclosure statement

No potential conflict of interest was reported by the author.

ORCID

Jean Beaman http://orcid.org/0000-0002-1645-0968

References

Alba, R. D., and N. Foner. 2015. *Strangers No More: Immigration and the Challenges of Integration in North America and Western Europe*. Princeton, NJ: Princeton University Press.

Almeida, D. 2017. "Exclusionary Secularism: The Front National and the Reinvention of Laïcité." *Modern & Contemporary France* 25 (3): 249–263. doi:10.1080/09639489.2016.1272561.

Ayling, P. 2017. "Whiteness as a Symbol of Quality Education: An Analysis of Perceptions of Quality Education among Affluent Nigerian Parents." Paper presented at the annual meeting of the British Sociological Association, Manchester, April 4-7.

Beaman, J. 2015. "Boundaries of Frenchness: Cultural Citizenship and France's Middle-Class North African Second Generation." *Identities: Global Studies in Culture and Power* 22 (1): 36–52. doi:10.1080/1070289X.2014.931235.

Beaman, J. 2017. *Citizen Outsider: Children of North African Immigrants in France*. Oakland, CA: University of California Press.

Beauchemin, C., C. Hamel, M. Lesne, and P. Simon. 2010. "Les Discriminations: Une Question De Minorites Visibles." Population & Societés (INED) 466. https://www.ined.fr/fichier/s_rubrique/19134/466.fr.pdf

Beydoun, K. A. 2013. "The French Kiss 'Race' Goodbye." *Al Jazeera*, June 2. http://www.aljazeera.com/indepth/opinion/2013/06/20136273349196523.html

Bonilla-Silva, E. 2012. "The Invisible Weight of Whiteness: The Racial Grammar of Everyday Life in Contemporary America." *Ethnic and Racial Studies* 35 (2): 173–194.

Bonnett, A. 1998. "Who Was White? the Disappearance of non-European White Identities and the Formation of European Racial Whiteness." *Ethnic and Racial Studies* 21 (6): 1029–1055. doi:10.1080/01419879808565651.

Byrne, B. 2007. "England – Whose England? Narratives of Nostalgia, Emptiness and Evasion in Imaginations of National Identity." *The Sociological Review* 55 (3): 509–530. doi:10.1111/j.1467-954X.2007.00720.x.

Chabal, E. 2015. *A Divided Republic: Nation, State and Citizenship in Contemporary France*. Cambridge: Cambridge University Press.

Cretton, V. Forthcoming. "Performing Whiteness: Racism, Skin Colour, and Identity in Western Switzerland." *Ethnic and Racial Studies*.

Emirbayer, M., and M. Desmond. 2015. *The Racial Order*. Chicago: University of Chicago Press.

Essed, P., and S. Trienekens. 2008. "'Who Wants to Feel White?' Race, Dutch Culture and Contested Identities." *Ethnic and Racial Studies* 31 (1): 52–72. doi:10.1080/01419870701538885.

Fanon, F. 1967. *Black Skin, White Masks*. New York: Grove Press.

Fleming, C. 2017. *Resurrecting Slavery: Racial Legacies and White Supremacy in France*. Philadelphia: Temple University Press.

Gallagher, C., and F. W. Twine. 2017. "From Wave to Tsunami: The Growth of Third Wave Whiteness." *Ethnic and Racial Studies* 40 (9): 1598–1603. doi:10.1080/01419870.2017.1308535.

Garner, S. 2016. *A Moral Economy of Whiteness: Four Frames of Racializing Discourse.* London: Routledge.
Garner, S. 2017. "Surfing the Third Wave of Whiteness Studies: Reflections on Twine and Gallagher." *Ethnic and Racial Studies* 40 (9): 1582–1597. doi:10.1080/01419870.2017.1300301.
Goldberg, D. T. 2006. "Racial Europeanization." *Ethnic and Racial Studies* 29 (2): 331–364. doi:10.1080/01419870500465611.
Goldberg, D. T. 2009. *The Threat of Race: Reflections on Racial Neoliberalism.* Malden, MA: Wiley-Blackwell.
Hall, S. 1991. "Old and New Identities, Old and New Ethnicities." In *Culture, Globalization, and the World System: Contemporary Conditions for the Representation of Identity*, edited by A. D. King, 44–68. Minneapolis: University of Minneapolis Press.
Harris, C. 1993. "Whiteness as Property." *Harvard Law Review* 106 (8): 1707–1791. doi:10.2307/1341787.
Hughey, M. 2010. "The (Dis)Similarities of White Racial Identities: The Conceptual Framework of 'Hegemonic Whiteness'." *Ethnic & Racial Studies* 33: 1289–1309. doi:10.1080/01419870903125069.
Jugé, T. S., and M. P. Perez. 2006. "The Modern Colonial Politics of Citizenship and Whiteness in France." *Social Identities* 12 (2): 187–212. doi:10.1080/13504630600583387.
Kastoryano, R. 2004. "Race and Ethnicity in France." In *Social Inequalities in Comparative Perspective*, edited by F. Devine, and M. C. Waters, 66–88. Malden, MA: Blackwell Publishers.
Kastoryano, R., and A. Escafré-Dublet. 2012. "France." In *Addressing Tolerance and Diversity Discourses in Europe: A Comparative Overview of 16 European Countries*, edited by R. Zapata-Barrero, and A. Triandafyllidou, 27–47. Barcelona: Barcelona Centre for International Affairs.
Kaufmann, E. 2006. "The Dominant Ethnic Moment: Towards the Abolition of Whiteness?" *Ethnicities* 6 (2): 231–253. doi:10.1177/1468796806063754.
Keaton, T. D. 2009. "'Black (American) Paris' and the 'Other France': The Race Question and Questioning Solidarity." In *Black Europe and the African Diaspora*, edited by D. C. Hine, T. D. Keaton, and S. Small, 95–118. Champaign: University of Illinois Press.
Keaton, T. D. 2010. "The Politics of Race-Blindness: (Anti) Blackness and Category-Blindness in Contemporary France." *Du Bois Review: Social Science Research on Race* 7 (1): 103–131. doi:10.1017/S1742058X10000202.
Keskinen, S. 2017. "Racialization, Minority Activism, and the Threat of Separatism." Paper presented at the British Sociological Association Annual Meeting, Manchester, UK.
Lentin, A. 2008. "Europe and the Silence about Race." *European Journal of Social Theory* 11 (4): 487–503. doi:10.1177/1368431008097008.
Lewis, A. 2004. "'What Group?' Studying Whites and Whiteness in the Era of 'Color-Blindness'." *Sociological Theory* 22 (4): 623–646. doi:10.1111/j.0735-2751.2004.00237.x.
Lombardo, P., and J. Pujol. 2011. "Le Niveau De Vie Des Descendants D'immigrés." In *Les revenus et le patrimoine des ménages*, 73–81. Paris: INSEE.
McCrone, D., and F. Bechhofer. 2010. "Claiming National Identity." *Ethnic and Racial Studies* 33 (6): 921–948. doi:10.1080/01419870903457199.

Meurs, D., A. Pailhé, and P. Simon. 2006. "The Persistence of Intergenerational Inequalities Linked to Immigration: Labor Market Outcomes for Immigrants and Their Descendants in France." *Population* 61 (5–6): 645–682. doi:10.3917/pope.605.0645.

Moschel, M. 2011. "Race in Mainland European Legal Analysis: Towards a European Critical Race Theory." *Ethnic and Racial Studies* 34 (10): 1648–1664. doi:10.1080/01419870.2011.566523.

Müller, U. A. 2011. "Far Away so Close: Race, Whiteness, and German Identity." *Identities* 18 (6): 620–645. doi:10.1080/1070289X.2011.672863.

Ndiaye, P. 2008. *La Condition noire: Essai sur une minorité française*. Paris: Editions Calmann-Lévy.

Noiriel, G. 1996. *The French Melting Pot*. Minneapolis: University of Minnesota Press.

Omi, M., and H. Winant. 1994. *Racial Formation in the United States: From the 1960s to the 1990s*. New York: Routledge.

Peabody, S., and T. Stovall, eds. 2003. *The Color of Liberty: Histories of Race in France*. Durham, NC: Duke University Press.

Silberman, R. 2011. "The Employment of Second Generations in France: The Republican Model and the November 2005 Riots." In *The Next Generation: Immigrant Youth in a Comparative Perspective*, edited by R. Alba, and M. C. Waters, 283–316. New York: New York University Press.

Silberman, R., R. Alba, and I. Fournier. 2007. "Segmented Assimilation in France? Discrimination in the Labor Market against the Second Generation." *Ethnic and Racial Studies* 30 (1): 1–27. doi:10.1080/01419870601006488.

Silverstein, P. 2008. "Thin Lines on the Pavement: The Racialization and Spatialization of Violence in Postcolonial (Sub)Urban France." In *Gendering Urban Space in the Middle East, South Asia, and Africa*, edited by K. Ali, and M. Rieker, 169–206. New York: Palgrave/Macmillan.

Simon, P. 2012. *French National Identity and Integration: Who Belongs to the National Community?* Washington, DC: Migration Policy Institute.

Strauss, A., and J. M. Corbin. 1990. *Basics of Qualitative Research: Grounded Theory Procedures and Techniques*. Thousand Oaks, CA: Sage Publications.

Tribalat, M. 2004. "An Estimation of the Foreign-origin Populations of France in 1999." *Population* 59 (1): 49–80. doi: 10.3917/pope.401.0049.

Trieu, M., and H. Lee. 2016. "Midwest Asian Americans, Internalized Racial Oppression, and Identity Shifts." Paper presented at Global Cities Symposium, Purdue University, October 17–18.

Twine, F. W., and C. Gallagher. 2008. "The Future of Whiteness: A Map of the 'Third Wave'." *Ethnic and Racial Studies* 3 (1): 4–24. doi:10.1080/01419870701538836.

Weiner, M. F. 2012. "Towards a Critical Global Race Theory." *Sociology Compass* 6 (4): 332–350. doi:10.1111/j.1751-9020.2012.00457.x.

Weiner, M. F. 2015. "Whitening a Diverse Dutch Classroom: White Cultural Discourses in an Amsterdam Primary School." *Ethnic and Racial Studies* 38 (2): 359–376. doi:10.1080/01419870.2014.894200.

Wieviorka, M. 1992. *La France raciste*. Paris: Éditions du Seuil.

The whiteness of cultural boundaries in France

Angéline Escafré-Dublet

ABSTRACT
This paper proposes to explore French cultural policy to show how the white boundary making is embedded in the 'routine structures' of cultural life. It takes the example of the implementation of national cultural policy as a means of seeing how the privilege of the majority operates. Against a formal insistence that the French definition of citizenship and equality does not leave room for the discussion of visible identities, it argues that immigration issues in relation to culture are relevant *loci* for the numerous instances of boundary drawings that it helps highlighting. Specifically, it shows how in the process of designing and implementing cultural policies, administrative officials have defined culture as artistic, universal and secular throughout the years. As a consequence of which, the privileged currently take part in the definition of artistic norms, while migration-related minorities have to justify for the social benefit of any of their artistic initiative.

Introduction

This paper proposes to explore French cultural policy to show how the white boundary making is embedded in the 'routine structures' of cultural life. It proceeds against a formal insistence that the French civic understanding of citizenship tends to confine the definition of identity to the vocabulary of colour-blindness. In his definition of the nation, Renan argued that citizenship in France was a 'daily plebiscite', which meant that anyone could belong to the nation, regardless of their race, religion or ethnicity, provided that they adhere to a set of civic values (Renan 1882). More contemporary debates tend to reassert this idea, albeit with a stronger emphasis on the necessity to adhere to civic values on the part of politicians, particularly that of *laïcité* (Sarkozy 2010). Nonetheless, there is a prevailing insistence that the definition of Frenchness is articulated in universalistic and civic terms, in ways that does not leave much room for the discussion of visible identities, not least whiteness as the most 'invisible' of all.

However, considerations over physical appearance and skin colour are not completely absent from the discussion on identity and nationality. The difference in experience between French people with a white European background and French people with a non-white background demonstrates the continuing salience of race in the Republic (Beauchemin, Hamel, and Simon 2016). As a result, French people who are 'not white' are more likely to declare that they are not seen as French by the rest of the society (Simon and Tiberj 2016).

As much as whiteness has been described as a kind of capital 'embedded in the routine structures of economic and political life' (Duster 2001), however, this should not overlook formal French cultural policy which represents an area of national cultural definition (Thiesse 2007), and so an integral part of France's national project. As such it is case in point for the study of matters related to culture that are not exclusively related to the management of the arts (Bennet 1992). This paper is based on an empirical enquiry into the archives of the French administration.[1] On one hand, the archives of the Ministry of Culture were scrutinised from its inception in 1959 to the emergence of its interest in 'cultures of immigration' (*cultures de l'immigration*) in the 1980s, with the aim to analyse the official mindset towards immigrants as an audience but also as creators of artistic forms of expressions. On the other hand, an inquiry into the archives of the administration in charge of immigrant population in the Social Affair and Labour Ministries, from its initial take on the issue with the creation of a dedicated department in 1958 (the Social Action Funds – *Fonds d'action sociale*) to its formal definition of a policy of integration at the end of the 1980s, allows for an insight into the ways in which culture has been called upon to solve issues related to social and economic integration. What do we mean by 'culture' when we talk about immigration in France? Is it the usual artistic productions that the Ministry of Culture is in charge of promoting or a way to differentiate immigrants from nationals? The comparison between two administrative cultures, one articulated around artistic criteria and the other one around social imperatives, provides for a vantage point to explore the meaning given to 'culture' when it comes to immigration over a period of rapid expansion: from 1962 to 1990, France went from 4.67% to 6.35% foreigners (National Census records). Finally, in terms of data collection, working documents of the administration were crossed with oral history interviews with administrative officials and non-governmental actors: artist, activists and curators ($n = 25$).

The paper proceeds in the following manner. First, the paper identifies the main obstacles associated with the study of whiteness in France, such as the specificities of the discussion on race and the predominant use of colour-blind categories of analysis. Second, it argues that immigration and (de-) colonisation are relevant *loci* to launch a discussion on whiteness for the numerous instances of boundary drawings that it helps highlighting. Third, it takes the concrete example of national cultural policies from the 1960s to the 1980s as a means of seeing how the privilege of the majority is to participate in the definition of artistic norms. By contrast, aesthetic criteria are not the norms for migration-related minorities. They often have to apply to alternative sources of funding and meet with other types of social criteria. The paper argues that a double standard in cultural policy implementation demonstrates an unequal treatment between a privileged majority and an underprivileged minority.

Using or not using the concept of whiteness in France

Race, racism and the colour-blind approach

Arguments against the notion of whiteness in France displays similar logic as to whether or not to register race. One of the most important arguments is that it is not grounded on historical facts. As opposed to the United States that instituted racial difference in its founding Naturalization Act of 1790 (all 'free white persons' can become an American citizen), Metropolitan France defined citizenship regardless of one's racial, religious or ethnic origin. While a racial order of things has been established in the French colonial empire; notably, slavery in the French colonies and a variety of different status for colonial subjects, a view was that what took place in the colonies, stayed in the colonies (Peabody and Stovall 2003). As evidence of this, black slaves were free when they were in the Metropole and the difference in status that was imposed on French Muslims in Algeria did not hold once they settled in Metropolitan France (Shepard 2006).

Another important argument is that it is illegal. Operating a distinction based on one's racial, ethnic or religious origin is incompatible with the notion of equality, even when it is in a situation to favour or promote a specific group, as in the case of an affirmative action policy (Sabbagh 2002). Visible identities are not considered as valid categories of identification, and among these visible identities, the category of white is even more valid, as it is deemed invisible. The legal impediment to ethnic categorisation makes it difficult to analyse the current state of facts (there is no such thing as a breakdown of the population according to racial category), hence why social scientists and political analysts favour the use of alternative categories of analysis that are much more meaningful in the French context, such as social or spatial categories (Beaud and Pialloux 1999). Further, general arguments against the use of the notion of whiteness or race point towards the idea that it is morally reprehensible. As much as using the term race is associated with the belief in racial hierarchy, the reifying power of identity categories is seen as something foreign that has nothing to do with French reality. This explains a regular practice of 'racial avoidance' (Bleich 2003, 14). Moreover, talking about whiteness might be perceived as giving legitimacy to conservative talk about anti-white feelings (Fleming 2017, 59).

The difficulties associated with the study of whiteness in France parallels in many respects those identified in the study of racial construction: it is often seen as giving way to an exclusionary discourse that sees identities as permanently attached and unmovable. It is morally reproved as antithetical to the liberating discourse of Republican equality.

The return of assimilation as white backlash

The historical argument against the study of whiteness has already been addressed in the literature. It has already been made clear that a discussion on whiteness does not only stem from a black and white post-segregation type of society such as the United States or South Africa. It has been transposed to a multicultural society where the definition of whiteness has extended. Discussion on whiteness has been linked to the notion of multiculturalism and a possible white backlash, i.e. a set of responses to equalities discourses as they unfolded from the 1960s to the 2000s (Hewitt 2005).

At the same time, equality discourses have unfolded differently from the 1960s to the 2000s in France although there was a notable exception in the early 1980s, when the socialist party adopted a 'differentialist' rhetoric (Silverstein 2004; Gordon 2012). When faced with the rising electoral success of the National Front that adopted an exclusionary stance, mainstream parties embraced a Republican consensus that reasserted the invisibility of difference in the public sphere. Since the late 1980s, the French official 'philosophy of integration' has focused on keeping racial, ethnic or religious differences in the private sphere (Favell 1998). Writing a common national narrative has implied a strong return to Republicanism (Chabal 2016). Moreover, the invisibility of difference is now regarded as the most inclusive strategy, i.e. the only way to preserve France from the divisive power of the extreme right (Brubaker 2001). This is not to say that France has been immune to the rise of the French National Front. The party's broad base is attested to by the fact that it consistently did better than any other far-right party in Europe throughout the 1990s and the 2000s (Klandermans and Mayer 2006). However, there is a strong consensus that the best solution to rising populism remains to keep a difference in the private sphere.

Moreover, the equivalent to a white backlash in France can be traced through the debate over the purported neglect of the 'poor Whites' in France (Laurent and Leclère 2013, 17). An import from the colonial context where they were opposed to rich colonial settlers, the category 'poor Whites' (*petits blancs*) is a rare use of a colour-code category in the French language that traces its origins in the colonial context. The addition of the 'poor' adjective (or rather 'little') underlines that whiteness is associated with wealth and privilege. The use of this category in the Metropolitan French debate is a sign that what happens in the colonies does not always stay in the colonies. Even though the term does not refer to an actual group living in Metropolitan France, the metaphorical use is an indication that colour, if not race, does matter.

Finally, the debate over the purported neglect of the white poor unfolds similarly to the discussion on a white backlash: it is based on the assumption that social policies in the past 20 years have been disproportionally favouring immigrants and is articulated through a critique of multiculturalism. Multiculturalism is understood as a foreign model implemented abroad that recognises the difference and promote the withdrawal into segregated communities. It results in the reaffirmation of the French model of integration, perceived as the only way to protect a society's threatened cultural integrity (Wieviorcka 2013).

Locating whiteness in France

Despite all these constraints the ways in which a racial frame has been used to highlight certain phenomenon calls for an *experimental* use of whiteness on the French case.

Whiteness as Frenchness?

In France, the historical construction of difference is articulated in national terms rather than according to a colour line. Whiteness is a 'by-product of Frenchness' (*sous-produit*) according to immigration historian Gérard Noiriel (2013). Arguably, most of the historiography has been articulated around the process of making foreigners 'into Frenchmen' (Weber 1976). In the *French Melting Pot*, Noiriel demonstrated the process by which various waves of immigrants settled and became French (1996). An important part of the book is dedicated to the invisibility of such a contribution to French society, what he calls a « denial of memory ». One argument for this invisibility can be found in the lack of data available to scholars: up until 1999, all immigrants who had naturalised appeared as French in census data (Simon 1998). The data impediment to researching immigrant life paths operated as a serious obstacle to the analysis of immigrant contribution to French society for a long time. In other words, becoming French is becoming *invisible* to the historian radar.

Moreover, the process of becoming French holds parallel logic to that of 'whitening' developed in American historiography. In *Whiteness of a different color* (1998), Matthew Frye Jacobson demonstrates how there was never such a thing as a permanent settlement on what it is to be black and what it is to be white, specifically with regards to the arrival of groups such as the Irish or the Italians who were Roman Catholic.

As much as a black and white order of things presided to the understanding of immigrant settlement in the US (Guglielmo 2003), the national vs. foreigner divide in France shaped the historical analysis of immigrant life path in France. As a result, an important part of the French scholarship on immigration history is articulated around the concepts of integration and naturalisation (Blanc-Chaléard 2000; Guery 2013). What is more, it is common to observe that the state invisibleness of some immigrant population is presented as an evidence of their integration. In a political context where cultural and religious differences are supposed to be strictly confined to the private sphere, the invisibility of immigrants is regarded as a sign of full assimilation.[2]

Whiteness does not equal Frenchness and discussing Frenchness cannot replace discussing whiteness in France, however. Empirical evidences show that whiteness forms *part* of discussing Frenchness actually (Beaman 2015; Mazouz 2017; Fassin 2010; Escafré-Dublet and Simon 2014). For instance, second-generation youth mention being denied membership to the national community – not being seen as French – based on their not being white: 'A French person who is not questioned whether he is French, is a French person who is white and has a French name' says a 24-year-old man of sub-Saharan descent during a 2009 qualitative survey on what it means to be French (Escafré-Dublet and Simon 2014, 78). Therefore, there is a racial construction of Frenchness that cannot be subsumed to the civic definition of French citizenship.

Working out whiteness: the colonial terrain

The literature on colonisation and immigration can be helpful in understanding the racialisation of Frenchness. Even though, under Napoleonic ruling, the colonial conquest of new territories implied the extension of French nationality to all colonised populations – colonised peoples became French and had no other nationality than that of the country that ruled over their territory[3] - colonial officers operated a distinction between the colonisers and the colonised for ease of administration. They introduced a distinction between nationality and citizenship in the colonies, although the two are otherwise compounded in France. It drew a clear boundary between who gets to be a French citizen: the colonisers but not the indigenous populations (Cooper 2014).

Status distinction resulted from the necessity of the Empire: maintaining control over subjected populations, but also a moral concern for racial mixing (Saada 2002, 99). The concern for racial mixing is a distinctive feature of racially segregated society, as demonstrated through miscegenation laws under Jim Crow in the United States. In the French colonies, it suggests ways of thinking about being French and being white that refers to the moral project of the civilising mission of the colonisers (Conklin 1997). Arguably, the legal concern for racial mixing was limited to the colonial context and the difference in status – and the Indigenous Code – never applied in the French Metropole, even during the time of the Empire (Shepard 2006). Nonetheless, historical inquiries have demonstrated the unequal treatment that colonial subjects received while they were in France. They were the target of specific surveillance in the context of the wars of decolonisation (Blanchard 2011). But also, systematically differentiated from the rest of the nationals when it came to housing, social welfare, labour and the collection of national census data (Bernardot 2008; Pitty 2006; Spire 2003; Escafré-Dublet, Kesztenbaum, and Simon 2018). In her historical inquiry on the French welfare state and Algerian families, Lyons argues that there is a continuity in how the civilising mission was conceived in the colonies and the way Algerian families were monitored in the Metropole (2013).

From these examples, (de-)colonisation and the implementation of public policy towards migrants, therefore, appear as a means of seeing processes of boundary drawing and racial differentiation in France.

Whiteness in France: privilege and cultural norms

That the definition of citizenship in France is civic makes no doubts in principle, it is in practice and in the 'structure of everyday life' however, that one may identify processes of boundary drawing that take their roots in the period of decolonisation and have been rearticulated in face of new challenges. In this process, culture is one of the interesting *loci* to look at (Cervulle 2013). The following takes the example of cultural policy design and implementation during and after decolonisation.

Race, racism and culture

As in most countries in Continental Europe, culture replaced race in France in the post-war period. The discredit on the biological understanding of difference consecutive to the crimes committed by the Nazi regime extended to a larger discredit put upon the category of race to analyse social processes (Lentin 2005). Instead of acknowledging a social construction of race as it is often the case in the United States or Great Britain, the race was permanently associated with a biological understanding of differences. In this process, culture (even more so than ethnicity) became the most privileged category in use to assess difference. In France, Levi-Strauss writings on Race and History (1952), and his argument that diversity is in no way the outcome of biological differences were particularly influential (Brattain 2007).

However, racism understood in the process of racialisation is also about culture. As argued by Modood, there exists a form of 'cultural racism' that 'naturalizes culture as if culture is automatically reproduced and does not change over time' (2005, 13). From this perspective 'racialization' does not require phenotypic difference but can also make use of or 'construct cultural traits as a basis of differentiation' (Halej 2012, 4). This is particularly the case when culture becomes the predominant category through which difference is assessed: what does it mean when culture is mentioned in the French context, and what does it mean when it is mentioned in link with migration-related diversity? The empirical analysis of French administration archives offers an insight into the official mindset towards the issue. Along with other scholars who call for 'putting policies into cultural studies' (Bennet 1992), I argue that analysing cultural policy implementation allows to highlight crucial dynamics with regards to politics and identity, beyond considerations limited to the management of arts. In the following, I argue that, when it comes to immigrants, culture is given a different meaning than the official one given for the rest of the population.

Culture as defined by the institution

Culture, as defined by the institution in France has an artistic meaning. This is mostly linked to the context of the creation of a Ministry of Culture in 1959. The first state entity to be dedicated to cultural policy, it emerged as a result of De Gaulle's decision to appoint his long-time friend and writer, André Malraux as 'Minister of Cultural Affairs'. Malraux himself was reported saying that he 'did not know what culture was' (*Le Monde*, 12 November 1963) and it was not clear what a Ministry of Culture should do (Lebovics 1999). Nonetheless, an administration was to be under the authority of the Minister, and this administration was broken down by art form: music, literature, theatre, cinema and fine arts. Some of these departments already existed but were scattered in various ministries, such as the department of Fine Arts – formerly in the Education Ministry or the one in charge of Cinema – formerly in the Industry Ministry (Urfalino 1996). As a result, the creation of a Ministry dedicated to cultural affairs participated in the process of state modernisation and rationalisation, characteristic of the post-war period. However, some other departments were created *ad hoc* such as the Theatre Department, which embodied a new state function: bringing culture to the people. The official mandate of the Ministry was to 'render accessible humanity's greatest masterpieces to the greatest possible number of French people' (Malraux 1959), and in this perspective, the theatre was thought to be the best medium to reach to the highest number of people, in and outside Paris. Malraux's mandate saw the establishment of theatres all around France, which were labelled Houses of Culture (*maisons de la culture*).

Culture, in the early years of the French Ministry of Cultural Affairs, was therefore associated with theatre and artists. This artistic meaning was confirmed in the following decades as cultural policy became an established field of public intervention, with a network of structures, a specific profession and a set of guidelines to monitor its implementation (Dubois 1999).

Moreover, cultural policies are part of national projects (Thiesse 2007). When De Gaulle gave the impetus to a ministry that was to oversee all cultural affairs on French metropolitan soil, his will was to unify the population in a common soul.

Culture was strategic all through the 1960s: higher officials from the Ministry sat in the strategic planning committee (*commissariat au plan*) and argued for the implementation of cultural policies as a tool for social development (Dubois 1999, 217). The rhetorical use of unity, humanity and commonality was recurrent in the working documents of the strategic planning committee and reveals the 'built-in-tendency towards cultural homogenization' that cultural policy displays in periods of national (re-)construction (Delhaye and Van de Venden 2014).[4]

Finally, with the establishment of culture as a field of public intervention, administrative officials in charge of monitoring cultural policy became art critique themselves. Even though the reasoning behind the creation of a dedicated Ministry for cultural affairs was a democratic one: to extend the access to cultural forms for the highest number of people. The mean through which this objective was pursued was nonetheless a top-down process: artistic value was defined at the top and the Ministry retained a function of 'cultural arbitrary' (Bourdieu and Passeron 1977).

Throughout the years, the French Ministry of culture extended its definition of artistic value, particularly at crucial moments such as in 1981 when Jack Lang became culture Minister of the newly elected Socialist President, François Mitterrand (Martin 2008). Nowadays, the Ministry is no longer the guardian of elite forms of culture but incorporates a wide array of cultural forms and structures – from museum and art schools to music venues and circus schools. However, in practice, the implementation of French cultural policy and the working habits of officials in the Ministry of Culture keeps a 'legitimist orientation' (Coulangeon 2016): the French Ministry of Culture, as main provider and organiser of French cultural life defines culture as artistic, universal and secular.

Culture as defined in relation to immigration

Culture, as it is mentioned above, does not get to be defined by the Ministry. When it does, it is often an inclusive and open definition that is given, mostly in link with the mandate of the Ministry that sees a universal message in humanity's masterpieces. Moreover, the French Ministry of Culture has long been involved in international cooperation with artists abroad and the French government was a key player in the adoption of the UNESCO Declaration for Cultural Diversity in 2003. There is no such thing as a rejection of foreign forms of art or foreign artists.

However, it is striking to observe that when they respond to the challenge of immigration in France, administrative officials in the Ministry often give indications of the different meaning they allocate to culture when in relation with immigration. In his analysis of ethnic groups and boundaries, Barth argues that 'the features which are taken into account are not the sum of the objective differences, but only those which the actors themselves regard as significant' (1969, 14). In this perspective, I argue that the reaction of the French Ministry of Culture to the question of immigration offers numerous instances of boundary drawing between the in-group and the out-group members.

Three decisive moments may be highlighted. The first decisive moment is at the creation of the Ministry of Cultural Affairs when Malraux recruited his main collaborators from high civil servants who had previously served in the colonies (Lebovics 1999). This choice was motivated by two factors. The first factor is related to the context of decolonisation. This was a new Ministry and high civil servants were not eager to come and serve in an administration that they were not sure would last and of which they knew little. Only colonial civil servants who were unemployed as a result of the dismantling of the French Empire could be less selective for their appointment. The second factor is linked to the role of culture in the civilising mission (Conklin 1997): the training of colonial civil servants was particularly strong in humanities, and Malraux could consider they were more expert on matters related to culture, than other civil servants with experience in mainland France (Rauch 1998). Some of them, such as Emile Biasini, had been developing cultural activities during their colonial appointment that Malraux regarded as valuable experience. According to Emile Biasini, Director of Theatres and Cultural Development from 1961 to 1966, André Malraux once said to him: 'What you did with Africans, why don't you come and do it in France' (Biasini 1995, 139).

The input of colonial officers at the inception of the Ministry of Culture contributed to a definition of artistic value in universalistic and colour-blind terms. Even though Emile Biasini was discharged after five years, his contribution was decisive in defining the ways in which the state should render accessible humanity's masterpieces. His opinion was to put people *in presence* of masterpieces, and the universal message would strike them. Known as *esthetic choc theory*, this strategy relies heavily on the preeminence of artistic value and the existence of universal artistic criteria. This first decisive moment shows the role of decolonisation – and the practical necessity to employ former colonial civil servants – in shaping the implementation of a cultural policy that defines art as universalistic and colour-blind at the time of its inception in 1959.

The second decisive moment is in the mid-1970s when the French government – like the British and the German governments at the same period – attempted to put a halt to economic migration. The design of a new policy to manage immigration flows consisted in the limitation of entrances and the suspension of residency titles, but it also encompassed the implementation of cultural programs that aimed at facilitating the integration of immigrants or their return home (SETI 1977). I argue that this contributed to the process of boundary drawing by selecting elements that were regarded as French, as opposed to others that were regarded as foreign or pertaining to 'origin countries'. In the process of designing and implementing a 'cultural policy adapted to immigrants', working documents of the administration shows that the Labor Ministry in charge of immigration regulation could not count on the contribution of the Ministry of Culture[5]: administrative officials from the Ministry of Culture did not join meetings, and when asked to support projects, their refusal shows that they considered immigrant projects as folkloric and far from meeting the artistic quality they expected from state-funded art. As a matter of fact, when looking at cultural programs towards immigrants designed by the Labour Ministry in charge of immigrant workers, they often operated within the framework of an anthropological definition of culture, ranging from language to cooking, including religious habits.[6] The differential meaning given to culture when it comes to immigration is visible in this choice.

The decision to include a cultural component in the making of immigration policies, in the 1970s, I argue, contributed to a definition of culture as anthropological in relation to immigration. That a more encompassing understanding of culture, which extends to the many meanings and signs that make sense to a group, may apply is not a problem *per se*. After all, it is closer to Levi-Strauss definition of culture, which was central to the rebuilding of France in the post-war period. However, that this anthropological meaning of culture only applies to foreign-born and that an artistic definition applies to nationals is more problematic. First, it is an evidence of the use of cultural practices as a basis of differentiation that parallels to a process of racialisation. Second, it suggests an unequal treatment that contradicts the Republican promise of equality. As long as immigrants' cultures are referred to according to the anthropological definition of culture, they are not acknowledged for their potential artistic quality and are restricted to their foreign status. In this second decisive moment, state-funded art appears as the norm against which others are judged and defined as different.

The third decisive moment is in the 1980s when cultural policy became a tool for immigrant integration. The decision to incorporate 'the cultures of immigration' (*les cultures de l'immigration*) in the scope of France cultural policy came along the general extension of the Socialist government's understanding of French national identity to regional and extra-territorial cultures (Martigny 2016). This more open, diverse and even multicultural approach to French identity was able to operate a breach in the administrative tradition to disregard migration-related projects.[7] Working papers of the Ministry of Culture and oral history interviews with former administrative officials shows that the experience of immigration became a valuable – sometimes even attractive – topic of artistic creation and interest to the institution.[8] However, the rise of an exclusive discourse on the right and the extreme-right of the political spectrum led to a transformation of the general approach to national identity. Towards the end of the 1980s, a 'Republican consensus' emerged (Weil 1992) that immigrants should integrate and that in this process, cultural programmes could help. Administrative officials in the Culture Ministry, together with their counterparts in the Social Affairs Ministry worked in defining guidelines for the implementation of cultural programmes that aimed at immigrant integration: they should reach to an audience usually isolated from cultural institutions, bridge with local NGOs and organise the mixing of different national groups.[9]

The reliance of the administration on cultural policy to solve matters related to immigration perception in political opinion shows that cultural policy serves to negotiate boundaries in France. In defining specific guidelines for the implementation of cultural programmes that aimed at immigrant integration, administrative officials operated a differential treatment between immigrants and nationals. They channelled artistic projects that had a link with immigration to be funded through specific schemes and meet specific guidelines that were not only artistic (Golub 2000, 85). A point not to be missed by numerous immigrant artists or immigrant groups who would criticise this double standard. How is it that when a group of immigrants has an artistic project, they have to meet some specific guidelines that are not based on artistic value but on the project's perspective in terms of social development? During the organisation of a major exhibition entitled Children of Immigration at Centre Georges Pompidou in 1984, sculptor Rachid Khimoune deplored the fact that he had been invited to show his work, because of his immigrant background and not because of his artistic merit (Escafré-Dublet 2009). This third decisive moment of the early 1980s, therefore, saw the reinforcement of a differential treatment between immigrant and non-immigrant forms of artistic expression despite a notable extension of cultural policy implementation.

Conclusion: cultural norms and whiteness

The differential treatment received by migration-related artistic projects allows us to identify the privilege embedded in the routine structure of cultural life: the privilege is to be evaluated according to the impartiality of aesthetic criteria, as opposed to having to justify for its social impact. The privilege of the majority is to be able to define culture in universalist terms, when minorities are constrained with end goals. Recent cut in cultural policy budget has increased this tendency. Local structures need to address issues such as *laïcité* or de-radicalisation in order to maintain their activities in disadvantaged neighbourhoods. One can observe a continuity between the 1980s, when cultural projects were called upon to solve issues related to social and economic integration, and the current situation when local NGOs are asked to propose projects that seek to foster French secularism and Republican values (CGET 2016). It all happens as if art had to prove itself more useful in some areas than others. Arguably, the function of culture for social development was at the core of the Ministry of Culture from its inception.

However, considering that some specific areas and some specific populations are the targets of such programmes reveal a double standard of implementation.

The literature on whiteness can help us reframe the discussion around inequality and difference. Instead of keeping the focus on systems of stigmatisation, it helps us shift our focus on the reverse: the definition of privilege. I argue that, in the French context of cultural policy, privilege is to be able to propose artistic projects and be evaluated according to their artistic value, in continuity with the principles that founded the Ministry of Culture in 1959, as opposed to having to justify for their social function. Whiteness can be defined as a 'site of elaboration of a range of cultural practices and identities, often unmarked and unnamed' (Frankenberg 2001). The lack of clear determination of what culture means in relation with immigration come through as a striking evidence of this asymmetrical relation.

Notes

1. For more details on archival records see (Escafré-Dublet 2014, 243–250).
2. The purported invisibility of Portuguese migrants is often interpreted as a sign of their integration in post-war France (Cordeiro 1999).
3. « …le pays conquis revêt (…) la nationalité du pays au profil duquel l'annexion est faite » Décision D., 1862-II-180 de la Cours d'Alger.
4. Sources: Archives of the Ministry of Cultural Affairs, 1959–1969: National Archives, 1995 0514, articles 1–11.
5. Sources: Archives of the Fund for the cultural intervention of the Ministry of Culture, 1971–1983: National Archives, 1985 0599, articles 1–165 and 2006 0272, articles 1–29; oral history interviews with administrative officials in the Ministry of Culture ($n = 6$).
6. Sources: Archives of the Direction for population and migration of the Labour Ministry, 1974–1981, 1985 0095, articles 1–5 and 1987 0440, articles 12–176 and 1989 0108, articles 91–98; oral history interviews with administrative officials in the Labour Ministry (n = 5).
7. Although only the term pluricultural (*pluriculturel*) can be found in official documents.
8. Sources: Archives of the Direction for cultural development of the Ministry of Culture, 1981–1986; interviews with administrative officials in the Ministry of Culture (n = 6).
9. Sources: Archives of the Social Action Fund, 1981–1996; interviews with administrative officials in the Social Action Fund (Ministry of Social Affairs).

Disclosure statement

No potential conflict of interest was reported by the author.

References

Barth, F. 1969. *Ethnic Groups and Boundaries: The Social Organization of Culture Difference*. Boston: Little, Brown.

Beaman, J. 2015. "Boundaries of Frenchness: Cultural Citizenship and France's Middle-Class North African Second-Generation." *Identities* 22 (1): 36–52. doi:10.1080/1070289X.2014.931235.

Beauchemin, C., C. Hamel, and P. Simon, eds. 2016. *Trajectoires et origines: Enquête sur la diversité des populations en France*. Paris: INED.

Beaud, S., and M. Pialloux. 1999. *Retour sur la condition ouvrière: Enquête aux usines Peugeot de Sochaux-Monbéliard*. Paris: La Découverte.

Bennet, T. 1992. "Putting Policy into Cultural Studies." In *Cultural Studies*, edited by L. Grossberg, C. Nelson, and P. Treichler. New York: Routledge.

Bernardot, M. 2008. *Loger Les Immigrés: La Sonacotra, 1956-2006*. Bellecombe-en-Bauges: Les Editions du Croquant.

Biasini, E. 1995. *Grands Travaux: De l'Afrique au Louvre*. Paris: Odile Jacob.

Blanc-Chaléard, M.-C. 2000. *Les Italiens dans l'Est parisien: Une histoire d'intégration (1880-1960)*. Rome: Ecole française de Rome.

Blanchard, E. 2011. *La police parisienne et les Algériens (1944-1962)*. Paris: Nouveau Monde éditions.

Bleich, E. 2003. *Race Politics in Britain and France: Ideas and Policy Making since the 1960s*. Cambridge: Cambridge University Press.

Bourdieu, P., and J.-C. Passeron. 1977. *Reproduction in Education, Society and Culture*. London: Sage.

Brattain, M. 2007. "Race, Racism, and Antiracism: UNESCO and the Politics of Presenting Science to the Postwar Public." *American Historical Review* 112: 213–232. doi:10.1086/ahr.112.5.1386.

Brubaker, R. 2001. "The Return of Assimilation? Changing Perspectives on Immigration and Its Sequels in France, Germany, and the United States." *Ethnic and Racial Studies* 24 (4). doi:10.1080/01419870120049770.

Cervulle, M. 2013. *Dans le blanc des yeux: Diversité, racisme et medias*. Paris: Editions d'Amsterdam.

CGET. 2016. *Secularism: A National Plan to Train Field Actors*. Paris: Commissariat general à l'égalité des territoires.

Chabal, E. 2016. *A Divided Republic. Nation, State and Citizenship in Contemporary France*. Cambridge: Cambridge University Press.

Conklin, A. 1997. *Mission to Civilize. The Republican Idea of Empire in France and West Africa, 1895-1930*. Stanford: Stanford University Press.

Cooper, F. 2014. *Citizenship between Empire and Nation: Remaking France and French Africa, 1945-1960*. Princeton: Princeton University Press.

Cordeiro, A. 1999. "Les Portugais une population ‹invisible›?" In *Immigration et intégration, l'état des savoirs*, edited by P. Dewitte, 106–111. Paris: La Découverte.

Coulangeon, P. 2016. "The Sociology of Cultural Participation in France 30 Years after 'Distinction'." In *Routledge Handbook of the Sociology of Art and Culture* edited by L. Hanquinet and M. Savage, 26-37.

Delhaye, C., and V. Van de Venden. 2014. "'A Commitment to Cultural Pluralism'. Diversity Practices in Two Amsterdam Venues: Paradiso and De Meervaart." *Identities* 21 (1): 75–91. doi:10.1080/1070289X.2013.828621.

Dubois, V. 1999. *La politique culturelle: Genèse d'une catégorie d' intervention publique*. Paris: Belin.

Duster, T. 2001. "The 'Morphing' Properties of Whiteness." In *The Making and Unmaking of Whiteness*, edited by B. Rasmussen, Klinenberg, and Nexica, 113-137. Durham: Duke University Press.
Escafré-Dublet, A. 2009. "Art, Power and Protest: Immigrants' Artistic Production and Political Mobilisation in France." *Diversities* 12 (1): 4–18.
Escafré-Dublet, A., and P. Simon. 2014. "Ce qu'il y a derrière l'identité nationale: L'appartenance face à l'altérisation." In *L'Identité Nationale: Instruments et Usages*, edited by C. Husson-Rochcongar and L. Jourdain, 63-80. Amiens: CURAPP.
Escafré-Dublet, A. 2014. *Culture Et Immigration. De La Question Sociale À L'enjeu Politique, 1958-2007*. Rennes: Presses universitaires de Rennes.
Escafré-Dublet, A., L. Kesztenbaum, and P. Simon. 2018. "La greffe coloniale en métropole. Les Français musulmans dans le recensement de 1954." *Sociétés contemporaines* 2 (110): 35–59. doi:10.3917/soco.110.0035.
Fassin, D., ed. 2010. *Les nouvelles frontières de la société française*. Paris: La Découverte.
Favell, A. 1998. *Philosophies of Integration: Immigration and the Idea of Citizenship in France and Britain*. London: Macmillan.
Fleming, C. 2017. *Resurrecting Slavery: Racial Legacies and White Supremacy in France*. Philadelphia: Temple University Press.
Frankenberg, R. 2001. "The Mirage of an Unmarked Whiteness." In *The Making and Unmaking of Whiteness*, edited by B. Rasmussen, W. Nexica, and Klinenberg, 72-96. Durham: Duke University Press.
Golub, A. 2000. "Cultures, culture, médiation. Police de l'art et des frontières." In *Cultures en Ville ou de l'art et du citadin*, edited by J. Métral, 89-100. La Tour d'Aigues: Les Editions de l'Aube.
Gordon, D. 2012. *Immigrants and Intellectuals: May '68 & the Rise of Anti-Racism in France*. London: Merlin Press.
Guery, L. 2013. *Le Genre De L'immigration Et De La Naturalisation. L'exemple De Marseille (1918-1940)*. Lyon: ENS Éditions.
Guglielmo, T. 2003. *White on Arrival. Italians, Race, Color, and Power in Chicago, 1890-1945*. Oxford: Oxford University Press.
Halej, J. 2012. "Through the Prism of Whiteness: Perception of East European Migrants in Britain." *Harvard Migration Workshop* 27 (March): 2012.
Hewitt, R. 2005. *White Backlash and the Politics of Multiculturalism*. Cambridge: Cambridge University Press.
Jacobson, M., and Frye. 1998. *Whiteness of a Different Color: European Immigrants and the Alchemy of Race*. Cambridge, MA: Havard University Press.
Klandermans, B., and N. Mayer, eds. 2006. *Extreme Right Activists in Europe: Through the Magnifying Glass*. Londres/New York: Routledge.
Laurent, S., and T. Leclère. 2013. *De quelle couleur sont les Blancs ?* Paris: La Découverte.
Lebovics, H. 1999. *Mona Lisa's Escort: André Malraux and the Reinvention of French Culture*. Ithaca: Cornelle University Press.
Lentin, A. 2005. *Racism and Anti-Racism in Europe*. London: Pluto Press.
Levi-Strauss, C. 1952. *Race and History*. Paris: U.N.E.S.C.O.
Lyons, A. 2013. *The Civilizing Mission in the Metropole: Algerian Families during Decolonization*. Stanford: Stanford University Press.
Malraux, A.1959. *Décret n° 59-889 portant organisation du ministère des Affaires culturelles*. Paris: Journal Officiel de la République française.
Martigny, V. 2016. *Culture(S) Et Identités Nationales, 1981-1995*. Paris: Presses de SciencesPo.

Martin, L. 2008. *Jack Lang, une vie entre culture et politique*. Paris: Flammarion.
Mazouz, S. 2017. *La République et ses autres. Politiques de l'altérité dans la France des années 2000*. Lyons: Presses de l'ENS.
Modood, T. 2005. *Multicultural Politics: Racism, Ethnicity and Muslims in Britain*. Edinburgh: Edinburg University Press.
Noiriel, G. 1996. *The French Melting Pot: Immigration, Citizenship, and National Identity*. Minneapolis: University of Minnesota Press.
Noiriel, G. 2013. "Il N'y a Pas De Question Blanche." *De quelle couleur sont les Blancs?* Paris: La Découverte.
Peabody, S., and T. Stovall. 2003. *The Color of Liberty: Histories of Race in France*. Durham: Duke University Press.
Pitty, L. 2006. "La main-d'œuvre algérienne dans l'industrie automobile (1945-1962), ou les oubliés de l'histoire." *Hommes et Migrations* 1263, 47-57.
Rauch, M.-A. 1998. *Le Bonheur d'entreprendre: Les administrateurs de la France d'outre-mer et le ministère des Affaires culturelles*. Paris: La Documentation française.
Renan, E. 1882. *Qu'est-ce qu'une nation?* Paris: Calman Levy.
Saada, E. 2002. "The Empire of Law. Dignity, Prestige and Domination in the 'Colonial Situation'." *French Politics, Culture & Society* 20 (2): 98–120. doi:10.3167/153763702782369795.
Sabbagh, D. 2002. "Affirmative Action at Science Po." *French, Politics Culture and Society* 2002, 52-64.
Sarkozy, N. 2010. *Discours de Grenoble*. Accessed on 04 April 2019 https://fr.wikisource.org/wiki/Discours_de_Grenoble,_par_Nicolas_Sarkozy
SETI (Secrétariat d'Etat aux travailleurs immigrés). 1977. *La Nouvelle politique d'immigration*. Paris: Secrétariat d'État aux travailleurs immigrés.
Shepard, T. 2006. *The Invention of Decolonization: The Algerian War and the Remaking of France*. Ithaca: Cornell University Press.
Silverstein, P. 2004. *Algeria in France: Transpolitics, Race and Nation*. Bloomingdale: University of Indiana Press.
Simon, P. 1998. "Nationalité et origine dans la statistique française: Les catégories ambiguës." *Population* 53 (3): 541–568. doi:10.2307/1534261.
Simon, P., and V. Tiberj. 2016. "Les registres de l'identité: Les immigrés et leurs descendants face à l'identité nationale." In *Trajectoires et Origines: Enquêtes sur la diversité des populations en France*, edited by Beauchemin et al., 531–558. Paris: INED.
Spire, A. 2003. "Semblables et pourtant différents. La citoyenneté paradoxale des "Français musulmans d'Algérie" en Métropole." *Genèses* 53 (Dec.): 48–68. doi:10.3917/gen.053.0048.
Thiesse, A.-M. 2007. *The Formation of National Identities », in the European Puzzle, the Political Structuring of Cultural Identities at a Time of Transition, In: Marion Demossier Ed*, 15–28. New York: Berghan Books.
Urfalino, P. 1996. *L'invention de la politique culturelle*. Paris: La Documentation Française.
Weber, E. 1976. *Peasants into Frenchmen. The Modernization of Rural France, 1870-1914*. Stanford: Stanford University Press.
Weil, P. 1992. *La France et ses étrangers: L'aventure d'une politique d'immigration*. 2005. Paris: Gallimard.
Wieviorcka, M. 2013. "A Critique of Integration." *Identities. Global Studies in Culture and Power*. 21: 633–641.

Reimagining racism: understanding the whiteness and nationhood strategies of British-born South Africans

Pauline Leonard

ABSTRACT
This paper explores strategies deployed by a sample of white, British-born South Africans to account for their positions during apartheid and post-apartheid. Whereas literature on white racism identifies denial as a key strategy towards racial discrimination and the maintenance of privilege, the historical and political 10 context of South Africa makes this tactic implausible. The paper contributes to understandings of pluralism within white identifications through investigation of diverse discursive strategies used to frame the overtly racist, apartheid regime and the present post-apartheid, supposedly, 'post-race' state. A range of positions attempting to minimise individual implication are identified. 15 A common feature however is to reimagine the structure of social relations in order to diminish responsibility for the sins of the past or the success of the future; suggesting profound difficulties in adjusting to the new social reality.

Introduction

> I didn't agree with some things that were going on, but I was visiting – whilst I came as a permanent resident with assisted passage, I was visiting. The first concept of apartheid in 1981 for me as a single white fellow is the bus goes past, that one's got black people on, this one's got white people on. And there's more black buses going past than there are white buses. Which annoyed me, because I would get on the black bus, they wouldn't worry me. (Stephen, 50, white)

As Stephen drove me through Johannesburg's affluent suburbs on our way to the old colonial Rand Club, I contemplated his positioning as a 'visitor' to South Africa. Stephen has lived in the city for 30 years, highly prosperous with children attending elite private schools. He appears thoroughly embedded in South

African life and takes an active interest in the nation's contemporary politics, albeit his descriptions of his lifestyle and his views on social relations in the post-apartheid regime appeared to be no different from earlier accounts of white lives under apartheid. I asked him what had changed since 1994, has South Africa successfully transitioned into Mandela's vision of a post-race 'rainbow nation'? 'We'll never quite get there, and never is a long time. You'll continue along this path, but you'll still have difficulty accepting some of the odd behaviour patterns or other parts of the community' he replies. Does this bother him? 'What have I got to lose?' he replies. 'You want to go back to the UK, you just book a flight. So, it doesn't seem like it's a big gamble to stay'.

The extent to which South Africa is transitioning into Mandela's vision of a racially equal society not only dominates South African politics but is of significant international interest, not least against the backdrop of rising white nationalist projects in the West (Garner 2017). Since the legal collapse of the racial segregation policies known as apartheid in 1994, and the privileges of white supremacism now officially rejected, South African people have been active in attempting to reform raced relations, facilitate greater economic and social equity and imagine new 'post-race' performances of nationhood and citizenship (Steyn and Ballard 2013; Conway and Leonard 2014). However, the considerable and impressive scholarship examining these processes of readjustment (e.g. Steyn 2001, 2012; Distiller and Steyn 2004; Ballard 2004a; Salusbury and Foster 2004; Steyn and Foster 2008) has revealed the extent to which whiteness has nevertheless sought to sustain its structurally privileged positionality (e.g. Ballard 2004b; Lemanski 2006; Dlanga 2016). Although formal policies no longer support racial segregation, racialised zones persist across the nation; economically, socially and spatially. While the complicity of white people in the perpetuation of this system is highly diverse, just how some continue to operate 'in the territory of being white' (Duster 2001, 15) within the changed regime remains an important question, not only when 'taking stock' of contemporary democratic South Africa (Steyn and Ballard 2013) but to furthering understandings of the complex and diverse ways in which white power and privilege live on, even when 'monolithic white supremacy is over' (Winant 1997, 76). Across the globe, whiteness not only continues to deliver entitlements but, in multiple contexts and political moments, is demonstrating a 'backlash' against the assumed gains of non-white Others (Hughey 2014; Garner 2017). To better understand and challenge the mechanisms by which white dominance is endlessly resincribed, its 'complex, multifaceted, contingent and fluid nature' (Watson, Howard-Wagner, and Spanierman 2015, xiv) continues to demand investigation in multiple and diverse contexts.

This paper aims to contribute to this interrogation by drawing on research of a sample of white, British-born, residents who first migrated to South Africa during the apartheid regime (1970s to 1980s) and who have since remained in the post-apartheid state. This group offers an interesting, if partial, lens to the questions raised above, with British migration to South Africa resulting from a long and highly specific political history. A tenet of both pro-imperial and Afrikaner Nationalist leaders, various schemes were designed from 1820 onwards to encourage British settlement (see Conway and Leonard 2014 for more detail). During the apartheid era, assisted passages were offered to white Britons as part of the government's attempts to shore up the racialised economy, such that Britons formed the largest national community of all white immigrants (averaging around 38% between 1946–87) (Peberdy 2009). At the height of white immigration (1961–77), 243,000 British citizens settled in South Africa. While the atrocities of late apartheid and perceived uncertainties about post-apartheid triggered an exodus of British and other white settlers, South Africa's attraction as a retirement destination has meant that numbers of British-born residents have stabilised at around 200,000 (Conway and Leonard 2014).

Migration during apartheid demanded that British migrants position themselves within a highly segregated context, overtly different from 'home'. Decisions had to be made anew on meanings of nationhood and white identities. In contrast to recent defences put forward by some South African-born whites (Steyn 2012), *ignorance* of apartheid was not a discourse available to this group. Nor, as suggested by other research on modern racism (Van Dijk 1992; Nelson 2013), was *denial* of racial discrimination. For whilst the representation of South Africa by the British media has been accused of 'structural hypocrisy' (Sanders 1999, 5), coverage of the black struggle had become increasingly mainstream from the 1970s onwards, escalating public campaigns to boycott sporting events and imported goods from South Africa (Fieldhouse 2005). It would have been difficult not to have been aware of the growing support for the anti-apartheid movement developing in Britain and internationally (Thörn 2006). At the same time, the coherence of whiteness was becoming contested in Britain, as black and Asian in-migration rose. Against a background of growing national debates on democracy, the meanings of race, racism and possibilities of multiculturalism, a decision was taken by this group to migrate to a hardened racist regime, where whiteness was explicitly mobilised as a resource in the securing of privilege. Migration was undoubtedly, therefore, bound up with choices about identities and performances of whiteness.

The decisions to be made were far from 'one off' but continued to need remaking. The apartheid state changed considerably between the 1960s and the 1980s: while in the 1960s and first half of the 1970s British migrants arrived at a country which was prosperous and, on the surface, economically and politically stable, from the late 1970s onwards the deepening entrenchment of racial segregation policies delivered political and economic turmoil (Conway and Leonard 2014). The increasingly challenging economic context and strengthening of black political action tested orthodoxies of whiteness, raising interrogations of its meanings and automatic relations with power and privilege (Steyn 2001). Indeed, the eventual ending of the apartheid regime occasioned 'a radical shift in identity construction among whites, whose comfortable social supremacy [became] discredited as racism' (Pillay and Durrheim 2013, 55). With whiteness publicly shamed and stigmatised (ibid), how white people position themselves within the new discursive terrain has been the subject of much critical investigation (Steyn 2004; Jansen 2009; McEwen 2013).

Research on racism more generally reveals that *denial* is a common white discourse, occurring at both the individual level as well as within institutional and political spheres (Nelson 2013). Studies across international contexts such as Australia, the Netherlands, Scotland and New Zealand identify that, within contemporary talk about race, denial of racism is a pervasive tactic to avoid charges of operating in racist terms (Van Dijk 1992; Augoustinos and Every 2007). This paper builds on these investigations, arguing that the South African context provides additional nuance in the identification of the discourses and tropes through which the territories of whiteness operate. While the persistence of overt racism within the nation challenges the ability of white people to position themselves within discourses of outright denial, the ways in which racialised systems, past and present are *reimagined* function to curate and sustain white subjectivities in relation to privilege.

Conceptualising whiteness in South Africa

While ever cautious of constructing an epistemology based on a form of 'exceptionalism' (Nuttall 2001, 116), the specificity of the South African historical and political context reveals how whiteness functions as a material and structural form of 'governmentality', 'a set of apparatuses and technologies, the aim of which is the regulation of the everyday perceptions, imaginations, and behaviours of people on a large scale' (Nuttall 2001, 118; Posel 2001). In apartheid South Africa for example, through a concatenation of discursive, institutional and legislative methods, the white state ensured that racial segregation was visibly and overtly embodied, performed and maintained through the material and cultural practices of everyday life (Posel 2001). As well as operating to govern others, whiteness also provides the apparatus for white people to manage themselves. However, whilst most research on white social positionality explores the strategies by which people secure advantage and maintain dominance (e.g. Ballard 2004b; Steyn and Foster 2008), it is also recognised that subjectivities of whiteness are multiple and complex, and that a range of alternative subject positions and performances co-exist (Nuttall and Michael 2000; Nuttall 2001; Twine and Gallagher 2008; Peens and Dubbeld 2013).

Some inspiring scholarship has identified how 'whiteness in South Africa differs from Western contexts in that it is more obvious in its potency: self-conscious rather than deliberately obscured and accepted rather than veiled as a site of privilege' (Salusbury and Foster 2004, 93). At the same time, it is recognised that 'whiteness in South Africa' is by no means a unified category, but is fractured historically, geographically, politically, religiously and economically as well as by language and (sometimes precarious) identifications with other nations (Steyn 2001). While some position themselves simply as 'South African', many also self-identify as Afrikaners, Russian Jews, Italians, Portuguese or British (Conway and Leonard 2014). Since the collapse of apartheid, and with it the singular, dominant 'master narrative' of whiteness, Steyn (2001) suggests that the diversities between performances of whiteness have become more multiple and nuanced. Politically and culturally, there now exist many shades of whiteness in South Africa.

That white identities are plural, dynamic, situationally and contextually produced, and subject to renegotiation, is well recognised in the Critical White Studies (CWS) literature (Frankenberg 1993; Bhopal 2018). The key point of interest here, making connections with this body of work but also contributing to its breadth of focus, is that post-apartheid South Africa is in a different historical and political moment to the contemporary dynamic of the North, where recent electoral and political events have demonstrated a noisy rise in the potency and open 'acceptability' of right-wing and populist mobilisation. Song (2014) argues that racialised discourse in the UK and the US is framed by 'a culture of racial equivalence', through which the playing field between whites and Others is deemed to have levelled or even tipped in favour of non-whites, and readjustment is thus sought (see also Garner 2017). While, as I go on to discuss, elements of this discourse certainly infuse the talk of white South Africans, this is against the dominant public discourse that apartheid, and the racial segregation and racism it spawned, has been universally condemned as a 'monstrous' regime. Here, whiteness has been very publicly disgraced and displaced, and the official political system is one of black rule (Pillay and Durrheim 2013).

A key focus of CWS in the North is to grapple with the ways in which normative (invisible) whiteness works to perpetuate embedded racism within its institutions (Rhodes 2013). For example, as stated above, Nelson (2013) argues that *denial* is a significant feature of modern racism. Building on Van Dijk's (1992) typology, she identifies four discourses by which denial of racism operates: temporal deflection: minorities today experience less racism than in the past; spatial deflection: racism is worse in other countries or regions; deflection from the mainstream: racism is only a problem with a small group of people; absence: outright dismissal of racism. While Nelson offers a valuable conceptualisation for the strategies of whiteness within these settings, the self-conscious and unveiled nature of South African whiteness (Salusbury and

Foster 2004) highlights the need for further granulation within frameworks of analysis, to understand 'the nuanced and locally specific ways in which whiteness as a form of power is deployed, performed, policed and reinvented (Twine and Gallagher 2008, 5) across both North and South. Within this mission, in the remaining sections of the paper, I explore the discourses mobilised by a sample of white British-born South Africans in their narratives of the changing political and social regime. I revisit 30 interviews which I conducted between 2009 and 2012[1] as part of a larger project exploring the meanings of whiteness in post-apartheid South Africa (Conway and Leonard 2014). Participants of both long and short-term residence were accessed through a combination of online advertising and snowballing under the banner of 'being British in South Africa'. The vast and speedy response we received revealed the traction that a British identity still holds for some, further supported through often very lengthy qualitative ethnographic and biographical interviews wherein participants talked openly about their attitudes and experiences. I am not, of course, claiming that these interviews are in any way representative of generalised attitudes of white British-born people in South Africa. Rather, the aim is to generate an intensive examination of a range of 'cultural voices' (Prasad 2005, 90) to develop theoretical understanding of their positions. The approach taken is to understand race, as with nationality and gender, as co-constructional, such that raced identities and positions are constructed and negotiated through social structures, interactions and practices, both discursive and material. The focus in this paper is the role of discourses or 'practices that systematically form the object of which they speak' (Foucault 1972, 49), and how, within this sample, these are deployed to make sense of the world by shaping meaning and, therefore, power relations.

Reimagining racial segregation

Through my thematic analysis of the interview transcripts, I identified four discourses by which respondents described their relationship to racial segregation and social transformation. What was striking were the ways in which racialised systems, past and present, were not denied, but reimagined and thus recast through the ways in which participants positioned historical and political events and their own role within these. Their discourses were in the main constructed at an individual level, although on occasion blurred into encompassing a broader social group of white people. Consequently, building on Nelson's (2013) typology of societal-level discourses, I categorise the four discourses as:

- *temporal reimagination*: racism in the past was not as bad as was made out and a return to the 'good old days' is desired by both blacks and whites,
- *boundary reimagination*: the racism of other groups (e.g. Afrikaners) is worse and racialised systems are a consequence of their beliefs, not ours,
- *acceptance*: racial segregation exists but is accepted as it delivers privileges to whites,
- *social reimagination*: racial segregation exists but social change is possible.

The discourses operated in an 'intertextualised' way: that is, people did not neatly position themselves within a single discourse but cross-currents of others were apparent (Baxter 2006). However, it was often the case that one discourse emerged as more significant in a respondent's story and so, in the following discussion, I draw on these as exemplifications.

Temporal reimagination

Steyn (2012) notes that some white South Africans claim ignorance of what was happening during apartheid, thus generating a 'feel-good' history for whites. While, as I explain above, it would have beggared belief for British migrants during the apartheid regime to claim ignorance of its existence, some I spoke to, through the strategy of *temporal reimagination*, attempted to recraft the past as 'not as bad as it was made out to be' in the British/world press. Moira, for example, migrating to South Africa in the late 1960s to establish a safari park, argued that what she found was actually no different from any other Western context:

> In some ways [the South African Government] were too good at communicating, because I don't think that racialism was any worse here, but the mistake was giving it a name: 'apartheid'. Rather than trying to shovel it under the carpet and say,' oh no, it doesn't exist', they were honest about it, upfront about it and said, 'yes it exists, we know it exists, we're going to support it and we're going to give it a name!'

It must be recognised that for those who arrived during the 1960s and early 70s, the apartheid system was at that time relatively 'low' compared to the heights of violence reached in the late 1970s and 1980s (Conway and Leonard 2014). Perhaps because of this, as well as the fact that whiteness in Britain was normalised and unacknowledged as a racial category, a key response among long-term residents, when asked about apartheid, was to attempt to de-problematise it by minimising its effects. Moira, for example, was keen to inform me that blacks and whites mixed freely and, further, that their access to space was no different to that of the whites:

> I used to go down into Pretoria, do my shopping and just window shop! And what fascinated me, I think more than anything else, was the fact that it was multi-racial, there were blacks and whites walking around without any obvious animosity and in fact, looking at some of the little black teenage girls walking around, they were better dressed than I was!

Moira's description of downtown Pretoria imagines an unracialised spatial freedom, despite the stringent pass laws which operated to regulate black access to urban space. Yet whilst the legal context is later acknowledged in Moira's narrative, its discriminatory nature is recreated:

> I was talking to this Afrikaner guy one day about blacks having passes, because this is something that always comes up, why do the blacks have to have passes? He put his hand in his pocket and he said, 'there's my pass, it's just that we call it an identity document'. Everyone had to have one, it wasn't just the blacks, and we still have to have them today. So, it wasn't just the blacks and the coloureds that had to have passes!

Steyn notes how 'white talk' 'undertakes ideological work to minimise damage to 'white privilege and maximise group advantage' (2004, 70) and it was clear from my interviews that, in relation to post-apartheid, the British-born South Africans I talked to were also adopting a set of tactical positions. Temporal reimagination featured as a trope, often mutating in the contemporary moment into a form of apartheid nostalgia: things were good under the system and most people, black and white, accept that its demise has therefore been 'a mistake'. Dick and Susan, for example, also in their seventies, are very comfortably settled in Kwazulu-Natal, surrounded by a community of other British-born residents and well looked after by their black 'helpers', Elijah and Christmas. Whilst local life generally passes peacefully, it is punctuated by the occasional violent incident, such as burglary and, occasionally, fatal attack. Susan thinks crime has got worse post-apartheid, and wonders, 'do we need a double-barrelled shotgun, just in case?':

> Elijah and Christmas say they were a lot better off under the Brittos, the white guys, because then – well there was law and order then you see. They had their dompas,[2] but they knew where they stood. It was interesting to hear them say that. Then they wouldn't get robbed on the way home for their wages as they might do now. There was more security because there was more control. I mean the police, you can't trust them now. And they [the blacks] suffer more than we do in many ways.

The major trope underpinning Susan's diatribe is the continued need for a strong, united white response to the violent onslaught which the ending of apartheid has unleashed against the white communities, myopically here conflated into 'the Brittos'. The material and legislative remnants of the old regime reimagined as a benign and secure system for both whites and blacks, continues to haunt and reanimate ideas about the community and nation that now exists. However, whilst this predominantly 'us' versus 'them' position has a clear resonance with the discourses of apartheid, by also claiming the existence of a *black* nostalgia for apartheid, a pseudo-racial solidarity is claimed to avoid any charge of racism (Van Dijk 1992).

Boundary reimagination

The second discourse constructed by participants was one of *boundary reimagination*: apartheid and its offspring, ongoing racialised zones in contemporary South Africa, are both 'nothing to do with me'. This strategy, demonstrated by Stephen's quote at the start of the paper, positions apartheid as the policy of an Afrikaans-led government, thereby displacing British-born whites into an alternative ('just visiting') community with little responsibility for its creation or demise. Boundary reimagination offers a position of marginality which can be simultaneously empowering: the problem of racism lies with others, allowing the British to position themselves within a 'myth of tolerance' (Essed 1991) and claim the moral high ground. Associated with this, most of the people I talked to had never become South African citizens and, as such, do not have the vote. A position of *'not political'*, disengaged from any sort of political participation or identification, was an almost ubiquitous and unsolicited ululation amongst respondents, of both long and short-term residence, often offered to justify their earlier tolerance of, or complicity with, apartheid and the privileges it delivered:

> 'I wasn't really interested in politics ... blow the politics! All my life, perhaps a terrible thing to admit, I haven't really been interested in people, what people do, how they act, what they do, let them get on with it, I'm just interested in having animals around. So, blow apartheid, I wanted an animal!' (Moira)

Similarly, the ongoing sustainability of racial segregation is attributed to the failing policies of the contemporary government rather than the actions of individuals. The supposed 'incompetence' of the African National Congress (ANC) to manage and run the country in accordance with the expectations of the 'first world' is a prevalent narrative which not only characterised the interviews but is also captured in the 'white talk' of the national press more broadly (Steyn and Foster 2008). Blaming the institutions of governance, while simultaneously disassociating themselves from these, is an important discursive tool to mitigate against accusations of personal acts of racism (Nelson 2013). British nationality was important here, frequently mobilised as part of the toolkit of boundary reimagination, whereby features of the current system were demonised as the behaviours of others. Neil, an engineer in his 40s illustrates:

There's a lot of corruption because there isn't the money or resources to give to people. One time I was driving back from work, and I was pulled over by a metro cop and he asked me questions like, "where you come from?" and then he says "it's Friday isn't it? I'm thinking I'm gonna have some beers tonight!" He was like, "do you have any money?" and it was like begging, begging ... police begging. It makes me annoyed and when I go to the UK and I see the police pull someone over, I feel like *that* is how it should be done, you know, not like what you see in this country.'

A challenge for white people in South Africa is managing the '"baggage" of the accumulated traces and relics of past selves while remaining virtuous through one's own continual reanimation' (Kelly and Riach 2014, 15). For many of my British respondents, this involved crafting the self carefully to dissociate from any sense of citizenship, and hence implication, in South African systems and processes, then and now.

Acceptance

In contradistinction, however, I found a distinctive feature of the talk of some was to openly acknowledge an *acceptance* of racial segregation. There was a classed and gendered aspect to this: South Africa's immigration policies under apartheid welcomed the skills of the (male) white working classes and British migrants suffering the economic volatilities of the 1970s and 1980s had much to gain in terms of occupational, career and, hence, class mobility (Peberdy 2009). Many were unapologetic of their acceptance of the system by which this was achieved. I chat to Richard, a retired manufacturer in his seventies, at a very exclusive and predominantly white Country Club in Johannesburg:

> I come from the East End of London, so there's a huge difference between where I was brought up to let's say, Port Elizabeth. So you're by the sea for a start. And the life, let's be honest about it, I'm not one of those people who will shrink form that part of South Africa's history, it was brilliant! If you come to a country where you've got blue skies and you've got sea and you've got beaches and you've got a wonderful way of life with a maid and everything is quite a zillion times cheaper than the UK; you think this is paradise! And it really was. So politics aside, there's nobody that was in that period from the '70s right up until '90s who can say that they didn't like the country, because it was very good to them at that time, let's make no bones about it.

In contrast to the fears that had escalated within white communities in the period leading up to 1994, daily lives and material circumstances have, for many whites, remained untouched. Kevin, a prosperous builder in his fifties explains:

> Sitting round the supper table, which we do a lot in South Africa, all the negativity! You know, "When the blacks come in this is going to happen, that's

going to happen". And nothing really changed. All that's changed is the word 'Apartheid' is not there. The whites still go to their pub, the blacks still go to their pubs. You've got the up-market restaurants where now, there's a mixture. But if I go around the corner to my local watering hole, I would say about 90%, 95% are whites. They tend to stick to where their friends are and what they want. So, in that way there's nothing changed much.

Kevin himself has strong working-class roots, having migrated in the 1980s from the depressed north-east of England looking for work. He draws on this background to justify why he quickly accepted the prevailing regime and the opportunities it offered for people like him. Now, 30 years later, he is the 'baas' of his own firm. Surveying his large house in the northern suburbs of Johannesburg, he rationalises: 'I could never have this lifestyle at home!' Stephen also enjoyed 'a bit of class-hopping' by coming to South Africa and realises how much he has benefited:

So occasionally I ask why I am still here. I know the answer, it's because my kids go to fantastic schools and I'm now fifty-something and have ten cars in the garage. There are things that you can do in a place like this that you cannot do in a place like London'.

Some respondents explained that although they *were* shocked when they first arrived in South Africa, they soon came to recognise how the system offered them substantial benefits. Jean (60s) confesses with some honesty:

What has struck my husband and I in later years is that it was very easy to accept the option that made life comfortable for us. So, one very easily forgot one's objections and accepted, accepted the status quo, because we were comfortable. Because of the townships and the locations, one didn't come into contact with a lot of black people, maybe the tea girl or the company driver, but you didn't meet very many black people, certainly not professional, middle-class people, they were all in exile, so one wasn't aware of what they were suffering, or what their problems were. And they didn't say much, I suppose they were frightened to, so we got on with our lives, and accepted what was really quite nice for us.

Jean now deplores her previous position and has tried to make amends by working actively within her local, mixed community. She explains that she is attempting to eschew the dualistic perspectives of 'us' and 'them' and adopt a more radicalised position towards South Africa's embedded racialisation.

Social reimagination

A minority of respondents took a position of *social reimagination* from the start, however. Their stories underline the diversity of positions and white subjectivities and how the experiences and ideas of white/British people in South Africa should not be conflated or foreclosed into a uniform 'condition' (Nuttall 2001). As Nuttall (2001) argues, the amplifications of forms of whiteness which may be at odds with the official orthodoxies must also be attended to. A salient illustration is provided by Andrew, an engineer who migrated to the Free State from London in the early 1980s, specifically to challenge apartheid. He remembers how it was 'such a different place to the UK':

> We were in a gold mining area, and there was absolutely no mixing between whites and blacks: it was very, very segregated, even the small shops, they'd have like the normal sort of white area and then a little sort of window with a ledge where the black people could go and buy their loaves of bread and things like that. That was a shock: a real eye-opener.

Andrew's job often took him into a black township near Johannesburg, which was unusual during apartheid:

> I used to go down to the black surveyor and the engineer, I could go round their houses because I had the permit to go into the township. Otherwise you didn't go into the township and you would get into trouble if you did ... it suited me actually, because it allowed me to see what I was really wanted to see. So, I was very lucky in that respect.

Andrew spent his evenings drinking in Soweto and soon made friends, despite the obstacles mixed relationships faced:

> If we wanted to socialise we'd go into Lesotho because there, there was no segregation. So, we, just like you would with any group of friends, you get in a minibus or a couple of cars or whatever and off you go. And I used to travel with them in the same vehicle, which might sound like it's nothing, but there were laws. We were often stopped by police on the way.

When Andrew met the woman who eventually became his wife, he continued to refuse to abide by the prevailing laws of the time and moved to live in Soweto:

> As a white man, a black woman was not allowed to ride in the front seat of a car, she had to go in the back seat. So driving around with my wife-to-be, we'd get stopped, and it would be, "What's she doing in there?" The police were pretty nasty. Gave you a hard time, I'd guess you'd say. I was rumoured to be one of perhaps two or three white people who were in one way or another living in Soweto. But I didn't think anything of it in those days. Didn't have any fear of getting into trouble or being caught doing something that I could be told off for. Didn't really cross my mind because it was like, well, that's what I wanted to find out about and I did.

For others, it has taken the post-apartheid context to force a rethinking of hegemonic assumptions and reimagine the society. As Jean explains: 'we all have weaknesses, we all make mistakes in life and we all have struggles, and we've had to change a lot. Coping with South African society is a huge challenge ... but we are trying to give back to the country something of the great benefits we've had'. Some of the newer migrants had come to South Africa specifically to be part of the changing regime and to witness history being made. Amongst these, there was an almost palpable sense of what could be achieved. Laura and her husband Matt, a missionary, had asked to be sent to Johannesburg, rather than Cape Town, so that they could live and work in the place 'where South Africa is really changing, where you're actually going to make a difference, really engage in South Africa!' Rejecting the northern suburbs where most white residents cluster, the couple live in Sophiatown, a black suburb which became legendary during the struggle. They are clearly enjoying being part of building a new society:

> 'there's a sense that everybody's invited to join in the history – you're very close to history being made here because it's in the making. You can taste it in your – that edge of meeting people. Everybody's making an effort and moving forwards – it's an opportunity – everyone says the opportunity is here to be grabbed and you're quite close to the people who are trying to grab the opportunities.'

Conclusion

Although apartheid ceased well over 20 years ago, this research shows how the regime's legacy continues to inflect the narratives of its sample of British-born South Africans, both in the re/making of memories about the past as well as in constructions of the present. The relationship with apartheid is complex: whilst it is clear that it was, and still is, a defining feature of their lives, for most there is a scant acknowledgment of any agency in its production. In contrast, a range of discursive techniques are deployed by which a position 'on the edge' is imagined. The aim is to remove themselves from the responsibility that accompanies power and privilege, and the centre of production of the trenchant racism from which they benefitted.

The discursive strategies are inventive. Key is the reimagining of the material realities and social relations of apartheid, claiming the system was subject to misrepresentation and exaggeration. Combined with the emphasis on British marginality in apartheid governance, the intention is to sidestep blame, and render unnecessary any need for engagement in, or support for, the struggle. In reconceptualising the streets of 1960s Pretoria, or the African bush, as spaces of pleasure, to be enjoyed equally by whites and blacks alike, the decision to migrate and settle in a highly racist and discriminatory regime is sanitised, even made rational. A similar, but more individualistic, tactic is to reimagine boundaries and position oneself as a 'visitor', a stranger in a foreign land, thereby locating apartheid as beyond the remit of personal responsibility.

Others openly admit the system was unfair and that they enjoyed its substantial material and social benefits. Whilst this goes some way to acknowledging complicity, by reifying apartheid rather than constituting it as a process which required ongoing participation and maintenance, a lack of responsibility for it is also negotiated. Those that claim that they tried to challenge apartheid, as well as support contemporary strategies for a racially equal society, still reveal a sense of entitlement to travel and live as they please.

The self-positioning of the British as *outside* of South African social structures and politics continues to dominate the narratives about the present. This disengagement and the lack of acknowledgement of the need to hold themselves and each other to account and critically challenge how their own practices may contribute to the ongoing production of privilege racism in South Africa is in itself a highly political and racialised act. It reinforces a position within the social structure of complicity with white privilege, tragically denuding British-born South Africans of the opportunity to reimagine the meanings of whiteness and nationhood in the post-apartheid context.

Notes

1. The larger research project, funded by the British Academy, was conducted with Daniel Conway. I focussed on British-born South Africans Johannesburg and Kwazulu-Natal and Daniel focussed on Cape Town.
2. Dompas, literally meaning 'dumb pass' were the pass books that black people were required to carry under apartheid.

Acknowledgments

Thank you to Daniel Conway, a wonderful friend and colleague, Nasar Meer for his support and collegiality, and the reviewers who helped the development of this article.

Disclosure statement

No potential conflict of interest was reported by the author.

Funding

The research was supported by the British Academy [grant number SG100009].

ORCID

Pauline Leonard http://orcid.org/0000-0002-8112-0631

References

Augoustinos, M., and D. Every. 2007. "The Language of 'race' and Prejudice." *Journal of Language and Social Psychology* 26 (2): 123–141. doi:10.1177/0261927X07300075.

Ballard, R. 2004a. "Assimilation, Emigration, Semigration and Integration: White People's Strategies for Finding a Comfort Zone in Post-Apartheid South Africa." In *Under Construction': Race and Identity in South Africa Today*, edited by N. Distiller, and M. Steyn, 51–67. Sandton, ZA: Heinemann.

Ballard, R. 2004b. "Middle Class Neighbourhoods or 'african Kraals'? the Impact of Informal Settlements and Vagrants on Post-Apartheid White Identity." *Urban Forum* 15 (1): 48–73. doi:10.1007/s12132-004-0009-1.

Baxter, J., ed. 2006. *Speaking Out: The Female Voice in Public Contexts*. Basingstoke: Palgrave Macmillan.

Bhopal, K. 2018. *White Privilege: The Myth of a Post-Racial Society*. Bristol Policy Press. doi:10.2307/j.ctt22h6r81.

Conway, D., and P. Leonard. 2014. *Migration, Space and Transnational Identities: The British in South Africa*. Basingstoke: Palgrave.

Distiller, N., and M. Steyn. 2004. *Under Construction': Race and Identity in South Africa Today*. Sandton, ZA: Heinemann.

Dlanga, K. 2016. "Only Whites Can End Racism." Accessed 28 April 2017. http://www.news24.com/Columnists/Khaya-Dlanga/only-whites-can-end-racism-20160708

Duster, T. 2001. "The "Morphing" of Properties of Whiteness." In *The Making and Unmaking of Whiteness*, edited by B. B. Rasmussen, E. Klinenberg, I. Nexica, and M. Wray, 113–137. Durham: Duke University Press.

Essed, P. 1991. *Understanding Everyday Racism: An Interdisciplinary Theory*. Thousand Oaks, CA: Sage.

Fieldhouse, R. 2005. *Anti-Apartheid: A History of the Movement in Britain*. Chippenham: Merlin.

Foucault, M. 1972. *The Archaeology of Knowledge and the Discourse on Language*. London: Routledge.

Frankenberg, R. 1993. *The Social Construction of Whiteness*. Minneapolis, MN: University of Wisconsin Press.

Garner, S. 2017. "Surfing the Third Wave of Whiteness Studies: Reflections on Twine and Gallagher." *Ethnic and Racial Studies* 40 (9): 1582–1597. doi:10.1080/01419870.2017.1300301.

Hughey, M. 2014. "White Backlash in the 'Postracial' United States." *Ethnic and Racial Studies* 27 (5): 721–730. doi:10.1080/01419870.2014.886710.

Jansen, J. 2009. *Knowledge in the Blood: How White Students Remember and Enact the Past*. Stanford: Stanford University Press.

Kelly, S., and K. Riach. 2014. "Monstrous Reanimation: Rethinking Organizational Death in the UK Financial Services Sector." *Culture and Organization* 20 (1): 7–22. doi:10.1080/14759551.2013.851678.

Lemanski, C. 2006. "Desegregation and Integration as Linked or Distinct? Evidence from a Previously 'white' Suburb in Post-apartheid Cape Town." *International Journal of Urban and Regional Research* 30 (3): 564–586. doi:10.1111/j.1468-2427.2006.00676.x.

McEwen, H. 2013. "Deserting Transformation: Heritage, Tourism and Hegemonic Spatiality in Prince. Albert *Diversities* 15 (2): 23–36.

Nelson, J. 2013. "Denial of Racism and Its Implications for Local Action." *Discourse and Society* 24 (1): 89–109. doi:10.1177/0957926512463635.

Nuttall, S. 2001. "Subjectivities of Whiteness." *African Studies Review* 44 (2): 115–140. doi:10.2307/525577.

Nuttall, S., and C.-A. Michael. 2000. *Senses of Culture: South African Culture Studies*. Oxford: Oxford University Press.

Peberdy, S. 2009. *Selecting Immigrants: National Identity and South Africa's Immigration Policies, 1910-2005.* Johannesburg, ZA: Wits University Press.

Peens, M., and B. Dubbeld. 2013. "Troubled Transformation: Whites, Welfare, and Reverse Racism in Contemporary Newcastle." *Diversities* 15 (2): 7–22.

Pillay, S., and K. Durrheim. 2013. "A Disgraced Whiteness: Tactics Used to Deny Racism, Reduce Stigma, and Elicit Sympathy." *Diversities* 15 (2): 53–65.

Posel, D. 2001. "Race as Common Sense: Racial Classification in Twentieth Century South Africa." *African Studies Review* 44 (2): 87–113. doi:10.2307/525576.

Prasad, P. 2005. *Crafting Qualitative Research: Working in the Postpositivisit Traditions.* New York: M E Sharpe.

Rhodes, J. 2013. "Remaking Whiteness in the "postracial" UK." In *The State of Race*, edited by N. Kapoor, V. S. Kalra, and J. Rhodes, 49–71. Basingstoke: Palgrave.

Salusbury, T., and D. Foster. 2004. "Rewriting WESSA Identity." In *'Under Construction': Race and Identity in South Africa Today*, edited by N. Distiller and M. Steyn, 93–109. Sandton, ZA: Heinemann.

Sanders, J. 1999. *South Africa and the International Media, 1972-1979: A Struggle for Representation.* London: Routledge.

Song, M. 2014. "Challenging a Culture of Racial Equivalence." *British Journal of Sociology* 65 (1): 107–129. doi:10.1111/1468-4446.12054.

Steyn, M. 2001. *Whiteness Just Isn't What It Used to Be: White Identity in a Changing South Africa.* Albany, NY: State University of New York Press.

Steyn, M. 2004. "Rehybridising the Creole: New South African Afrikaners." In *'Under Construction': Race and Identity in South Africa Today*, edited by N. Distiller and M. Steyn, 70–85. Sandton, ZA: Heinemann.

Steyn, M. 2012. "The Ignorance Contract: Recollections of Apartheid Childhoods and the Construction of Epistemologies of Ignorance." *Identities: Global Studies in Culture and Power* 19 (1): 8–25. doi:10.1080/1070289X.2012.672840.

Steyn, M., and D. Foster. 2008. "Repertoires for Talking White: Resistant Whiteness in Post-Apartheid South Africa." *Ethnic and Racial Studies* 31 (1): 25–51. doi:10.1080/01419870701538851.

Steyn, M., and R. Ballard. 2013. "Diversity and Small-Town Spaces in Post-Apartheid South Africa: An Introduction." *Diversities* 15 (2): 1–5.

Thörn, H. 2006. "Solidarity across Border: The Transnational Anti-Apartheid Movement." *Voluntas* 17: 285–301. doi:10.1007/s11266-006-9023-3.

Twine, F., and C. Gallagher. 2008. "The Future of Whiteness: A Map of the "third Wave"." *Ethnic and Racial Studies* 31 (1): 4–24. doi:10.1080/01419870701538836.

Van Dijk, T. 1992. "Discourse and the Denial of Racism." *Discourse and Society* 3 (1): 87–118. doi:10.1177/0957926592003001005.

Watson, V., Howard-Wagner, D., and Spanierman, L., eds. 2015. *Unveiling Whiteness in the Twenty-First Century Global Manifestations, Transdisciplinary Interventions.* Lanham: Lexington Books.

Winant, H. 1997. "Behind Blue Eyes: Whiteness and Contemporary US Racial Politics." *New Left Review* 225 (September–October): 73–88.

Securing whiteness?: Critical Race Theory (CRT) and the securitization of Muslims in education

Damian Breen ⓘ and Nasar Meer

ABSTRACT
This article revisits Critical Race Theory and brings it's explanatory capacity to bear on the contemporary racialization of Muslims in Europe, most specifically the experience of British Muslim communities in education. The article argues that CRT can provide a theoretically fruitful means of gauging the ways in which anti-Muslim discrimination might be engendered through various strategies around securitization. In a social and political context characterized by a hyper-vigilance of Muslim educators in particular, the article concludes that applying CRT allows us to explore how a general latent whiteness is given political content through a particular racialization of Muslims.

Introduction

'While this appears to be an attack on a particular community, like the terrible attacks in Manchester, Westminster and London Bridge it is also an assault on all our shared values of tolerance, freedom and respect'.[1] So stated London Mayor Sadiq Khan in the aftermath to the terrorist attack by a white nationalist on Finsbury Park Mosque. That it needs to be specified that the safety and security of Muslim Britons is coterminous with the safety and security of non-Muslim Britons, suggests that something is out of kilter with how we have come to approach the topic of security. Indeed, and while there is now a critically compelling literature on the role and function of recent approaches to security in Britain (Holmwood and O'Toole 2017; O'Toole and Meer et al., 2016; Jackson 2015; Husband and Alam 2011; Kundani, 2009), the policy approach has remained strikingly asymmetrical in focusing upon the safety and security of the white majority, and what Muslim communities can better do to ensure this. This is despite the evidence that Muslims too are the victims of terrorism in the UK, whomever it is perpetrated by (Ismail 2017).

In this article we seek to advance a conceptual discussion of this topic, specifically bringing to bear literatures from Critical Race Theory (CRT) to show how our understanding of the securitisation of Muslims would benefit from a better foregrounding of the role and function of whiteness. It is argued that re-visiting and utilising CRT can encourage us to think about the ways in which 'security' in Britain has become encoded in notions of civic participation and national belonging, which are in turn anchored in repertoires of whiteness. The article illustrates this by examining the policy debates about 'Fundamental British Values' and the 'Trojan Horse letter'. Each example, it is argued, illustrates how majoritarian codes are crafting strategies that in effect police Muslim mobilisations and claims-making, most apparently in our cases in the field of education. Whose security is being elevated, we suggest, flows from priorities forged in latent assumptions of whiteness.

Critical Race Theory and whiteness

The provenance of Critical Race Theory may be traced to American legal discourse, in terms of 'a counter-legal scholarship to the positivist and liberal legal discourse of civil rights' (Ladson-Billings 1998, 7), and so foregrounds a concern with the historical, political and socio-economic position of African Americans relative to white American society. Relationality to whiteness, therefore, has always been central to CRT approaches, and specifically how this relationship is contoured by questions of 'race' and power. This is not intended as a benign description. The cornerstone of CRT approaches has been that 'racism is normal, not aberrant, in American society' (Delgado 1995, xiv). The 'normalisation' here, in Delgado's (1995, xiv) classic text *Critical Race Theory: The Cutting Edge*, casts racism as having formed 'an ingrained feature of our landscape, [where] it looks ordinary and natural to persons in the culture'. He continued:

> Formal equal opportunity rules and laws that insist on treating Blacks and whites (for example) alike, can thus remedy only the more extreme and shocking sorts of injustice... Formal equality can do little about the business-as-usual forms of racism that people of color confront every day and that account for much misery, alienation, and despair.

Perhaps an under-recognised feature of this process, is the notion of a wider *social desensitization* to racism; possibly signalled in Delgado's description of racism as 'business as usual'. A similar set of social processes are arguably characterised by other authors in their discussion of 'everyday racism' (Essed 1991) and the subjective negotiation of this. What we maintain is presently overlooked relates to how 'desensitisation' in turn increases the thresholds for what constitutes 'real' racism. This is perhaps what Goldberg (2006, 339) gestures to as the phenomenology of 'race' disappearing 'into the seams of sociality, invisibly holding the social fabric together even as it tears apart'. While policies promoting anti-racism continue to exist in society, they become focused on addressing unambiguous forms of racism, which incrementally normalises what ought to be considered extreme. So running parallel to observations about desensitisation, CRT scholars have long been interested in the nature and function of 'smokescreens' so called.

There are perhaps conceptual and empirical gaps here, and the CRT literature struggles with the more ambivalent mechanics of racialization, for much of the CRT literature works with a broad brush in typically centring on the ways racial justice is 'embraced in the American mainstream in terms that excluded radical and fundamental challenges to status quo institutional practices' (Crenshaw et al. 1995, xiv). This is understandable since CRT scholars do not have to work hard to elaborate how the US was founded in ways that relied on treating Black African slaves as property, and then formally emancipated African-Americans as socially, politically and legally lesser to whites (Ladson-Billings 1998, 15). American CRT theorists have been enmeshed in these debates and commenced with the implications of these historical relationships, before advancing the more normative position that a failure to question and acknowledge the function of racism is synonymous with acting to maintain the marginalised position of racialised minorities (Preston and Chadderton 2012). Much of this turns on the conviction that both tangible and intangible forms of racism are the principal means through which whiteness continues to be privileged.

Before we elaborate why this focus is useful in understanding the codification of security in Britain, specifically in terms of relationality to whiteness, it is important to register the divergences in thinking about whiteness. These correspond to its study from contexts marked by historical segregation (e.g. the US and South Africa) and elsewhere that whiteness has either (i) functioned (at least formally) as a banal repository of white majority conceptions of the given identity of societies, or (ii) ordered social relations in colonial states occupied overseas. What each reading shares in common, however, is that while whiteness was once 'seen as both invisible and normative, as being a state of "racelessness", this is increasingly recognised only as *appearing* to be the case' (Rhodes 2013, 52).

This paper is principally interested in the first kind, and proceeds with the distinction between whiteness and white individuals that has been usefully elaborated in well-known arguments by Bonnett (1997) and Leonardo (2002) respectively. For the latter, 'whilst whiteness represents a racial discourse, the category of white people represents a socially constructed identity usually based on skin colour' (Leonardo 2002: 31). Bonnett (1997: 189) meanwhile highlights both the distinction and relationship between white people and whiteness further, while Gillborn (2005) draws on Bonnett's argument to argue it is not necessarily the case that white people as individuals inevitably reinforce whiteness any more than heterosexuals are necessarily homophobic or men are necessarily sexist. The likelihood however is that most homophobic individuals are heterosexual, and most sexist discrimination occurs against women. This point is simply that whiteness as a racial discourse does not necessarily require white people to act in the interests of reinforcing whiteness. Equally, this means is that individuals do not have to be 'white people' to actively reinforce and act in the interests of whiteness.

Building on the distinction between white people and whiteness, Preston and Chadderton (2012, 92) move to think about this in terms of white positionality but register that this is also informed by intersectionalities across social class, gender, sexuality and ability/disability. Thus, 'temporary ambiguities' may occur where white people are positioned on the margins of whiteness. If this is so, the critical focus on whiteness in CRT is not an assault on white people but on the socially constructed and constantly reinforced power of white identifications and interests (Gillborn 2005, 488). Furthermore, Preston and Chadderton (2012, 92) condense extensive inquiry into the distinction between whiteness and white people through arguing that the many and various ways in which the white working classes, white immigrants and white women have been positioned on the fringes of white respectability are key examples where these groups are given a liminal position within whiteness (see also Nayak 2011). How and in what ways therefore does this characterisation of whiteness informed by CRT help shed light on security approaches in Britain?

Codifying whiteness in fundamental british values

One of the key sites for the application and development of CRT in the UK context has been within education (see Gillborn 2009; Rollock 2012; Chakrabarty 2012; Breen 2018; Bhopal and Rhamie 2014). The ways in which CRT has been applied to education within the UK are well documented elsewhere, and so this article does not replicate that work. The work of Gillborn in particular has drawn attention to the outcomes of policies designed and implemented by white power holders (Gillborn 2005). These strategies are premised on the notion of maintaining inequalities at the biting point of tolerable discomfort for marginalised racialised communities (Breen 2018, 51). Such policies operate under a veil of 'tacit intentionality' whereby policies which have a proven record of producing detrimental outcomes for racial minorities are advocated even in the light of evidence that they foster racial inequalities. For example, high-stakes testing, school performance tables and selection by 'ability' have remained within the British educational system for sustained periods of time in spite of the fact that research indicates that these policies have detrimental outcomes for black students (Gillborn 2005).

Work in recent years has started to apply CRT across minority ethnic groups in Britain, with emergent scholarly work on Muslim communities gaining momentum (see Housee 2012; Breen 2016, 2018). These developments raise new challenges around the scope of CRT, some of which are discussed throughout the remainder of this article. It is also important to emphasise that the enquiry here goes beyond education policy, yet this remains one of the key sites where intersections of stakeholdership in national identity for British Muslims, and strategies for securitisation have become increasingly central. Take for example the UK Government's commitment to *Fundamental British Values* (DfE 2015). Clearly, issues here around 'values' and national identity are complex, not only in their relation to each other, but also in terms of the implicit parameters for stakeholdership in national identification. Applying CRT to explore the implications of FBV for British Muslims therefore requires an analytically sensitive approach. The first way to address this is to think about whiteness as a series of racialized cultural codes rather than phenotype, and specifically how these codes are bound up with particularistic sets of public policy norms. In our reading this represents one such cluster of codes whose primary function is to reaffirm qualities of Britishness and national identity, but in a way that has specific implications for what FBV means in particular for British Muslims.

To step back, FBV and its manifestation in schools provides an interesting case within which the relationship between religiosity and perceived risks of extremism can be explored. Furthermore, the development of FBV and the duty to promote them within schools reveals the differential ways in which the broadly Christian heritage of the wider white population has been positioned within its framework, compared with how FBV impacts on Muslims in schools. FBV is an emergent phenomenon which has been most substantively manifested in the Department for Education's (DfE) Promoting fundamental British values as part of 'Spiritual, Moral, Social and Cultural' development (SMSC) in schools (DfE 2014). FBV actually first appears in political discourse in 2011 within the definition of 'extremism' outlined in the Government's counter-terrorism Prevent strategy:

> Extremism is vocal or active opposition to fundamental British values, including democracy, the rule of law, individual liberty and mutual respect and tolerance of different faiths and beliefs. We also include in our definition of extremism calls for the death of members of our armed forces, whether in this country or overseas (Prevent 2011, 107).

This definition of FBV would be referred to later in the 2011 Teacher's standards, which identified that upholding the standards included 'not undermining the fundamental British values, including democracy, the rule of law individual liberty and mutual respect and tolerance of different faiths and beliefs' (DfE 2011: 14). In June 2014 it was stated that then education secretary Michael Gove had announced that all schools would be required to promote FBV (Wintour 2014), with the publication of statutory guidance through SMSC following in November 2014 (DfE 2014). The implicit connection between FBV, SMSC and Prevent was a narrative about the security dangers posed by 'Islamic radicalism', and which became solidified in the revised Prevent duty guidance (2015) that explicitly used FBV within the definition of extremism.

The relationship between Prevent and FBV assumes that the values identified as British are self-evidently inherent, uncontested and forged against the threat of prevalent Islam in the public square. There are several problems with this, not least that part of FBV advocates for 'religious tolerance' (DfE 2011: 14). Yet FBV is clearly rooted in Prevent and fears around 'Islamic radicalism' (Prevent 2015). These fears are based on notions of increasing Islam in the public sphere as threat (see Breen 2018, 55), and arguably represent a clear example of *religious intolerance*. Aside from this contradiction, there is another problem here in the (re)establishment of particular values as being fundamentally British through FBV which would have previously been presented as shared values as part of engagement with SMSC. This affirmation of majoritarian cultural markers has thus become a default measure for identifying, by way of contrast, a definition of extremism. It is an approach that invariably cements the purpose of FBV as a strategy to police Muslim mobilisations and claims-making, perhaps most obviously apparent in the field of education. For example, the identification of SMSC as the primary mechanism within which the promotion of FBV has strategic and far-reaching implications, as the statutory duty to promote Fundamental British Values applies to both independent and maintained schools. In particular, the most recently Revised Prevent duty guidance for England and Wales (2015) states that:

> Independent schools set their own curriculum but must comply with the Independent School Standards, which include a specific requirement to promote Fundamental British Values as part of broader requirements relating to the quality of education and to promoting the spiritual, moral, cultural and cultural development of pupils. These standards also apply to academies (other than 16–19 academies), including free schools, as they are independent schools (DfE 2015, 10).

There are likely interesting reasons as to why the requirement to promote FBV extends beyond state-funded schools. Whilst there are numbers of Muslim schools in the state sector, these numbers are relatively low at 21, compared with 158 in the independent sector (Breen 2016, 11). Thus, for FBV to be effective in policing both values promoted in state schools with high proportions of Muslim pupils *and* Muslim faith schools, it has to be applicable across both independent and state sectors. This ensures a totality of duty to promote FBV as a strategy for policing not only all Muslims in *state* schools in England and Wales, but is also Muslim schools in the *independent* sector.

Trojan horse and responses: FBV and muslims in schools

It was perhaps no coincidence that the statutory duty to promote FBV followed concerns raised by the delivery of the anonymous 'Trojan Horse letter' to Birmingham City Council in November 2013 (Kershaw 2014, 3). The letter famously made claims about an alleged plot by some Muslim groups to install governors at schools in an 'Islamic takeover plot' (Mackie 2014). Whilst a series of investigations have followed, findings appear to be less than clear cut, with the Kershaw enquiry ruling that there was 'no clear and concerted plot', but that unorthodox methods may have been used by some stakeholders. In stark contrast, in July 2014 the newly appointed Secretary of State for Education, Nicky Morgan, addressed the House of Commons with the findings of Peter Clarke's inquiry (Clarke 2014) which indicated evidence of an 'aggressive Islamist agenda' (Coughlan 2014). Within this context it is pertinent to identify that Clarke had previously been Head of Counter Terrorism at the Metropolitan Police, and was appointed as Education Commissioner despite a lack of experience in the education sector itself. Clearly, with contradicting narratives emerging around the Trojan Horse letter, it is difficult to establish a clear understanding of how far the concerns raised were realised.

In the immediate aftermath of the letter, then Education secretary Michael Gove instructed the schools in Birmingham with a majority Muslim cohort to be inspected (Miah 2017: 87), even though only six schools were named in the Trojan Horse letter (Clarke 2014, 107). Yet, a series of OFSTED inspections followed in a total of 21 schools which had a majority intake of Muslim pupils (Miah 2017: 89). The subsequent emphasis on FBV within Prevent was introduced with the 'Common Inspection Framework' (OFSTED 2015) from September 2015 (Miah 2017: 101). Interestingly, the 21 inspections of schools in Birmingham appear to focus on section 10 of the Prevent strategy rather than the criteria present in OFSTED inspection guidelines in use at the time which had no key focus on preventing violent extremism (Miah 2017: 101), The implications of the above can be more concretely explored when looking at the role of OFSTED in the framing and reframing of activities documented in the schools inspected following Trojan Horse. For example, Oldknow School was inspected in January 2013 and rated 'outstanding' overall, and in relation to each of the four main criteria which include 'behaviour and safety of pupils' and 'leadership and management' (OFSTED 2013). Many areas of provision were praised, including an international school trip to Saudi Arabia, which was reported as a 'life changing experience' for pupils who had taken part (OFSTED 2013, 6). Furthermore, the school was also praised for using its funding to subsidise 'uniforms, trips and even large scale trips, such as the ones to Saudi Arabia, to ensure that any pupil is able to participate' (OFSTED 2013, 7).

Following the naming of the school in relation to Trojan Horse, the school was inspected again in April 2014. This time the school was rated overall as 'inadequate', with 'behaviour and safety of pupils' and 'leadership and management' also rated as 'inadequate' (OFSTED report 2014a). The change in rating, in and of itself, raises question as to the extent to which OFSTED exercised consistency in two reports less than eighteen months apart. However, the most striking revision was manifested in concerns around the previously highly praised trip to Saudi Arabia. In particular, the use of funding to subsidise the trip was questioned on the grounds that this had been used for Muslim pupils, and that the 'choice of destination meant that pupils from other faiths were not able to join the trip' (OFSTED 2014a, 7).

More worryingly, narratives around the Park View School raise further concerns about the consistency with which OFSTED have approached inspections following Trojan Horse. The school received a rating of outstanding in 2012, with the former Chief Inspector of Schools, Sir Michael Willshaw, praising the school's extraordinary exam success despite having 60% of its pupils qualifying for free school meals (Adams 2014a). Following the identification of Park View school, along with two other schools in the Park View Academy Trust, the OFSTED report for 2014 rated the school as inadequate. Whilst pupil attainment and quality of teaching were rated 'good', concerns were raised about the 'behaviour and safety of pupils' and 'leadership and management' which were both rated as 'inadequate' (OFSTED 2014b). However, a leaked report based on an inspection conducted on the 5th and 6th of March 2014, widely circulated within the government, made a series of relatively minor recommendations which included improving systems for safeguarding and strategies to ensure students are safe from extremism (Adams 2014a). This initial report would have lowered the overall rating to 'requires improvement', but under OFSTED rules the school would have retained its 'outstanding' rating due to its success in other areas (Adams 2014a). However, OFSTED inspectors returned to the school unannounced on the 17th of March 2014 to conduct a second inspection which ruled the school to be 'inadequate'. The implications of this rating were that the school would be placed into 'special measures', stripped of its governors and managing trust, and handed over to new and approved management (Adams 2014a). This would come a little more than two years after OFSTED inspectors rated the school as outstanding in all areas and praised it for its excellent academic results and inclusivity (Adams 2014b)

The confusion around the consistency of OFSTED procedures around Park View school was met with concern by both the Park View Educational Trust

(PVET) and assistant principal at the time Lee Donaghy. Writing for the *Guardian* newspaper in June 2014, Donaghy argued that a strongly held belief among staff was 'that the inspectors were ordered back into the school by somebody who felt that Park View had to be placed in special measures to enable the removal of Park View Educational Trust' (Donaghy 2014). Indeed, the initial leaked inspection report would have allowed the school to retain its governors and managing trust, but the second report ensured the removal of the Park View Educational Trust (PVET). The trust argued that there was a feeling of OFSTED 'working to a timeline and in a climate of suspicion, driven by the Trojan Horse letter and coupled with unproven allegations about Park View that had started to appear in the media' (PVET 2014). Park View school was subsequently renamed the 'Rockwood Academy', and is now sponsored by the CORE educational trust. Interestingly, along with Park View school, the Nansen primary school and Golden Hillock were also placed into special measures following their OSTED respective inspections in April 2014. All three were operated by the PVET, and the rating of these schools as 'inadequate' also allowed the Department for Education to remove the trust from the running of those schools and replace their governors (Adams 2014b). Nansen primary school is now affiliated with the CORE educational trust which replaced the PVET as sponsors at Park View school. In response, Sir Tim Brighouse, a former chief education officer in Birmingham, along with 20 co-signatories, expressed serious concern around the consistency of inspection procedures following Trojan Horse. In a letter to *The Guardian* in 2014 Brighouse et al stated:

> It is beyond belief that schools which were judged less than a year ago to be outstanding are now widely reported as 'inadequate', despite having the same curriculum, the same students, the same leadership team and the same governing body. This is uncharted territory, with OFSTED being guided by an ideology at odds with the traditional British values which schools are meant to espouse, particularly fairness, justice and respect for others (Brighouse et al cited in Adams 2014c).

The removal of the PVET as sponsors at Park View school, the Nansen primary school and Golden Hillock was met with a statement from the organisation which contested many of the grounds on which its schools had been rated as 'inadequate'. The PVET emphasised that 'the OFSTED reports find absolutely no evidence of extremism or an imposition of strict Islamic practices in our schools' (PVET 2014). Further to this, the Trust argued that 'the idea of a Trojan Horse plot has created a perfect storm for individuals and organisations with agendas around education, immigration, faith, securitisation and straightforward party politics' (PVET 2014).

Some of the wider problems around the way that Trojan Horse was handled are inherently related with contested ideas of what constitutes appropriate religious influence. All schools (whether denominational or not) are duty bound to provide Religious Education (RE) and collective worship (DfE 1994). The designation of RE and collective worship is subject to the local authority Standard Advisory Councils for Religious Education (SACREs). For non-denominational schools, RE and collective worship should be of a 'broadly Christian character' (DfE 1994). However, the SACRE for Birmingham had developed a multi-faith approach since 2007, which promoted RE in line with a multiplicity of religions given the diversity of the city (Birmingham City Council 2007). It was broadly ignored in the handling of the Trojan Horse case, that the schools named in the Trojan Horse letter were adhering to locally agreed RE syllabi and provision for Islamic collective worship. However, the Clarke report identifies that the focus of the investigation was on a small number of schools which had 'converted to academy status in recent years' (Clarke 2014, 7) At no point in the Kershaw or Clarke reports is it emphasised that the schools involved were adhering to all legislative requirements and arrangements previously in place – criteria on which they had been previously praised. There are two main problems here. The first is that what is locally upheld as good practice in multi-faith provision is overlooked by the DFE. The second, is that the lack of acknowledgement of the commitment to multi-faith principles in the local SACRE itself allows for a dramatic distortion of the accusations around the extent to which appropriate religious influence may have been exceeded. If we return to the wider concerns expressed around FBV and SMSC above, Trojan Horse represents an interesting case which draws attention to the privileging of white interests through explicitly demarcating appropriate *Islamic* influence from appropriate religious influence more generally.

In addition to the inconsistencies around Ofsted inspections inconsistencies were also found across a series of Hearings conducted by the National College for Teaching and Leadership (NCTL) investigating individual teachers following Trojan Horse. The furore around these investigations mirrored a broader moral panic where it was reported in the media that the NCTL were looking into around 30 teachers with a total number of 100 being possibly targeted (Holmwood and O'Toole 2017, 199). In reality, cases were actually brought against 12 individuals through a series of 4 Hearings by the NCTL (ibid.). A series of problems ensued, including concerns that witness statements which had been given to the Clarke report had been significantly longer and contained evidence which was favourable to the defence, but which had been omitted from both the report and statements elicited by the NCTL (Holmwood and O'Toole 2017, 201). Procedural irregularities continued, with Hearing 2 being quashed under a High Court appeal, in part due to failure to disclose evidence which was presented in Hearing 1 (Holmwood and O'Toole 2017, 200). The collapse of Hearing 1 followed on the grounds of irregularities which represented an 'abuse of the process which is of such seriousness that it offends the Panel's sense of justice and propriety' (Holmwood and O'Toole 2017, 202). This marked the end of the NCTL investigations, with only 1 teacher sanctioned with a 5 year ban, and the reasons given for the Panel to discontinue the main hearing make up 28 pages of text, alongside a Note submitted by the NCTL which acknowledged that the defence lawyers had been 'deliberately misled' (ibid). These examples demonstrate the ways in which Muslims have been differentially targeted through various different mechanisms of state apparatus around securitisation. But they also demonstrate that Muslims have been afforded differential access to due process through formal channels which have consistently facilitated strategic efforts to manipulate outcomes in the wake of Trojan Horse.

FBV and interest convergence

What the discussion thus far helps make apparent are the ways that strategies of securitisation have implications for the marginalisation of Muslim groups in Britain. If this process occurs at primarily the macro level, where such strategies are bound up with national protection, then a question remains around the interests of British Muslims within this dynamic. Specifically, the extent to which British Muslims figure as stakeholders in this process is missing, and assume indifference towards the interests of Muslims as requiring security too. Whilst the interests of British Muslims may well be entirely convergent with those of white English groups, the framing of approaches to securitisation arguably ignores this convergence. This process inevitably raises questions about the neutrality behind strategies for securitisation.

Derek Bell (1980) once argued that advances in US civil rights were concessions that aligned not with the objectives of civil rights, but with US propaganda efforts with the Soviet Union. It was an assertion empirically explored by Dudziack (2000) who pointed to newly available records of how the Supreme Court considered the cold war implications of their rulings in favour of civil rights cases. For CRT scholars, these concessions also came with a wider set of implicit demands, as Delgado (2003:129) put it, that 'African Americans and other people of colour...embrace anti-communism, fight in foreign wars, and purge themselves of radical elements'. For Bell, Delgado, Dudziack and others, the interests of minority ethnic groups were advocated or advanced only in so far as they converged with the interests that brought gains for white groups. What is overlooked here is that interest convergence should be read solely in terms of conventional social policy, but also as a means of supporting discursive facets of systems of injustice.

The UK has seen a great deal of new policy and practice informed by a concern with Muslim radicalism. Currently, the Prevent Duty requires frontline personnel to be vigilant for signs of increased religiosity, as though this were a reliable indicator of tendencies toward violence. As O'Toole (2015) summaries, public sector workers are being asked to interpret signs of radicalisation, based on a weak and contested understanding of radicalisation. One of the keys ways that this has been manifested is through recent revisions to Prevent. In 2011, the Prevent strategy was expressly revised to target 'non-violent extremism' on the theory that it is the precursor to terrorist activity (OSJI 2016: 33). Furthermore, the Revised Prevent Duty Guidance requires specified authorities, which includes schools, to prevent individuals from being drawn into both non-violent and violent extremism (for a full list of 'specified authorities' see Schedule 6 of the *Counter-Terrorism and Security Act, 2015*). It has been argued that the focus on 'pre-criminality', non-violent 'extremism', and opposition to 'British values' is fundamentally flawed (OSJI 2016: 34) for a series of reasons but two are most relevant here. Firstly, the success of the strategy is predicated on the assumption that its use can effectively determine whether an individual will commit a terrorist act in the future (ibid). Secondly, and related closely to this, the duty to report on 'pre-criminality' gives legal backing to potentially discriminatory determinations of 'extremism' by frontline professionals.

These concerns have indeed played out, with a significant number of children and young people being referred to the Government's de-radicalisation 'Channel' programme. For example, in 2015/16 56% of referrals were for individuals under 20, with the education sector making the most referrals (2,539) accounting for 33% of all referrals that year (Home Office 2017: 4). 65% (4,997) were referred for concerns related to Islamist extremism with 36% of those referred in 2015/16 (2,766) leaving the process requiring no further action. 3,793 (50%) were signposted to alternative services and 1,072 (14%) were deemed suitable, through preliminary assessment, to be discussed at a Channel panel (Home Office 2017: 4). The vast majority (76%) of those discussed at a Channel panel were regarding Islamic extremism. For 2015/16 381 individuals received channel support following a channel panel with 96% of these (365) subsequently leaving the process and 4% (16 individuals) receiving continued support (Home Office 2017: 4). Of those who left the process, 83% were identified as having their risk of being drawn into terrorism being 'significantly reduced' (Home Office 2017: 4). These figures could be taken to indicate that this process successfully rehabilitates individuals who would have otherwise committed terrible acts. But they could also be taken to demonstrate just how widely the net is cast when using tentative notions of 'pre-criminal' behaviour, and just how vague the criteria for referral is, given that only 4% of those who received support following a Channel panel required ongoing support. For 2015/16, only 16 individuals required ongoing support out of a total of 7631. Expressed as a percentage this amounts to 0.2% of all referrals, a statistic which might as easily be explained by a lack of rationale for 99.8% of referrals as by potential risk of committing a crime.

A number of case studies around referrals to the Channel programme give reason for concern. For example, in one instance a mother was called in to a nursery to discuss a picture their child had drawn of its father cutting a cucumber. When asked what the picture was of, the child was misinterpreted as saying 'cooker bomb' when attempting to say 'cucumber' (OSJI 2016: 72). The child's mother was then repeatedly told by the nursery manager that she had been referred to Channel, and that there was no opportunity to discuss and resolve the matter in-house adding 'you can prove yourself innocent. They might not take your kids off you' (OSJI 2016: 72). After refusing to sign the form and seeking legal advice, it transpired that she had not in fact been referred, but the process left her feeling 'like an outsider', and targeted as a result of being Muslim (OSJI 2016: 73).

In another case a Muslim kitchen staff member in one school drew attention to other kitchen staff neglecting the designation of utensils for serving halal food. This resulted in accusations from other kitchen staff that their Muslim colleague had said that she 'supported ISIS' and she was subjected to a disciplinary panel and subsequent appeals panel with the school and the Local Authority. Whilst the accused member of staff won the decision at the appeals panel and was reinstated, she was still issued with a 'first warning' and had not returned to work in the five months following this (OSJI 2016: 68). This brings us back the discursive positioning of British Muslims as stakeholders within strategies for securitisation. How do their interests figure and to what extent are they afforded legitimacy?

In the aftermath of the attack in Manchester on the 22nd of May 2017, various media sources drew attention to emergent accounts of Muslims contacting authorities over a period of time about radicalisation in Manchester. Mohammed Shafiq, Chief Executive of the Manchester-based 'Ramadhan Foundation', spoke specifically about anxieties members of the Muslim community had raised about Salman Abedi: 'people in the community expressed concerns about the way this man was behaving and reported it in the right way using the right channels', but 'did not hear anything since' (Mendick et al. 2017). Friends of Abedi also allegedly became so worried about his behaviour that they individually called the counter-terrorism hotline five years ago and again last year; they had been concerned that 'he was supporting terrorism' and had expressed the view that 'being a suicide bomber was ok' (Mendick et al. 2017). A member of the close-knit Libyan community in South Manchester also stated that Abedi had been banned from Didsbury Mosque after confronting an Imam who was delivering an anti-extremism sermon (Mendick et al 2017). The Mosque reported Abedi to the authorities and he had subsequently been placed on a 'watch list' because of his extremist views (Mendick et al 2017).

Muslim community engagement with counter-terror processes and procedures represents an example of interest convergence as British Muslims had clearly exercised serious concern as stakeholders in national security. Counter to the subtext of strategies like FBV, this represents an example of increased Islamic influence actually *informing* action around maintaining convergent interests around the protection of the public from violent extremism. There is evidence to suggest that Muslims were concerned about Abedi over a period of at least five years. Furthermore, the 2017 special report by the *Intelligence and Security Committee of Parliament* identified a range of areas where MI5 and counter-terrorism police could have taken more action (see ISC 2017). The question to ask at this point is whether or not more substantive action would have been taken had the voices informing concern been those of white, non-Muslim citizens.

The examples of innocent Muslims caught up in the Prevent strategy would suggest that this would likely have been the case, and clearly requires further and substantive empirical research. However, the framing of securitisation as a manifestation of ostensively white majority interests raises questions about the impact of racialisation on the legitimacy of voices in discourses around securitisation. Not only is securitisation principally associated with protection from Muslims, but in spite of active engagement, it still seems that concerns raised by Muslims have not been treated with urgency and legitimacy. Paying attention to the discursive features overlooked by CRT leads us to understand the positioning of Muslim voices as peripheral to those of 'real' stakeholders in securitisation. This example clearly demonstrates the intersection of interests around securitisation across white majority and Muslim minority groups. The intersection of these interests reveal differential expectations for Muslim and white English groups around the purpose of securitisation. Whilst public policy discourses around securitisation are firmly rooted in notions of protection for citizens, the wider expectations for Muslims in securitisation appears to be less about being protected and more about being active in engaging with counter-terror processes. This demonstrates a privileging of perceptions of security among white citizens at the expense of full stakeholdership in protection for Muslims.

Conclusion: securing whiteness

In a typically perceptive discussion of trajectories in the scholarship of whiteness studies, Garner (2017, 1585) argued that 'the sword of Damocles hanging over the scholar of whiteness is the question of how to wrestle its meanings into connection with other social relationships…and remaining true to the first wave origin: *make white supremacy visible*' (original emphases). This article is subject to these dynamics too, in so far as it has aimed to explore the ways in which reinvigorations of whiteness sit at an interplay between strategies around securitisation and what this means for Muslims in Britain. We have argued that the relationship between FBV and definitions of 'extremism' in the Prevent strategy has had profound implications for the monitoring and regulating of Muslim mobilisations in Britain.

The literature on Critical Race Studies allows us to see how FBV represents a majoritarian set of cultural markers, which assume a self-evident and inherent nature, uncontested and forged against the threat of prevalent Islam in the public square. For Muslims, misalignment with these markers has specific implications and specific risks are faced which do not apply to other Britons, most notably that of being associated with, affiliated with, or suspected of 'extremism'. In particular, one of the contributions made in this article has been to explore how the statutory duty to promote FBV manifests a particular approach for regulating Muslims in educational settings. Trojan Horse represents the starkest example of this, and further cemented public anxieties toward Muslims in the wider public consciousness. Further to this, the series of events around Trojan horse and the subsequent OFSTED inspections and reports discussed in this article demonstrate that anxieties around extremism exist on two levels – anxieties around extremism itself; and anxieties within regulatory authorities around being seen to have 'missed' a possible cause for concern relative for Prevent, SMSC or FBV. The case of Park View School and apparent inconsistencies in a series of OFSTED reports and inspections at the school seems to embody this process most substantively among the observations presented in this article.

Then, there is the question of what all of the above means for Muslims in Britain and their stakeholdership in national security. A series of processes have led us to argue here that securitisation, as it has played out in the British context, has an innate relationship with whiteness and resurgences in nationalist discourse in the English public space in particular. It goes without saying that there is clearly a need for further research in this area, but the theoretical considerations and empirical observations discussed in this article reveal how a complex interplay of public discourse, state strategy and implementation suggest that securitisation is about 'securing whiteness' in a series of ways.

Whilst the surface narrative suggests an impartial strategy for preventing violent extremism, our reading of how this is playing out reveals a far subtler and discursive effort to delineate 'British' and Muslim which has consequences for the latter. FBV is a set codes whose primary function is to reaffirm qualities of Britishness and national identity in a way that has specific implications for British Muslims. There is undoubtedly an implicit narrative around the threat of 'Islamic radicalism' that connects FBV, SMSC and Prevent. These efforts to reify Britishness have heralded a dynamic in which the reification of Britishness occurs where the interests of British Muslims as stakeholders in both nation and national security are diminished. The danger here is that the outcomes of these strategies could sustain a focus on issues around the fringes of radicalisation, rather than allowing a meaningful exploration for how the dynamics of these related strategies might contribute to feeling of alienation for Muslims as stakeholders in securitisation themselves.

Disclosure statement

No potential conflict of interest was reported by the authors.

Note

1. http://metro.cc.uk/2017/06/19/sadiq-khan-leads-calls-for-calm-in-wake-of-finsbury-park-terror-attack-6718247/ We are grateful to Claire Alexander for making us aware of this reference.

ORCID

Damian Breen http://orcid.org/0000-0001-9417-1027

References

Adams, R. 2014a. "Ofsted Inspectors Make U-Turn on 'Trojan Horse' School, Leak Shows." *The Guardian*, 30 May 2014, last accessed: 15/ 08/2017 https://www.theguardian.com/education/2014/may/30/ofsted-u-turn-trojan-horse-park-view-school-leak

Adams, R. 2014b. "Six Birmingham Schools Face Censure by Ofsted after Trojan Horse Inquiry." 1 June 2014, last accessed: 15/ 08/2017 https://www.theguardian.com/education/2014/jun/01/six-birmingham-schools-ofsted-special-measures

Adams, R. 2014c.. "Education Experts Voice Fury over Ofsted'S 'Trojan Horse' Schools Inquiry." *The Guardian*, 3 June 2014, last accessed: 15/ 08/2017 https://www.theguardian.com/education/2014/jun/03/education-experts-ofsted-trojan-horse-birmingham-schools

Bell, D. 1980. "Brown V. Board of Education and the Interest-Convergence Dilemma." *Harvard Law Review* 93: 518–533. doi:10.2307/1340546.

Bhopal, K., and J. Rhamie. 2014. "'Initial Teacher Training: Understanding 'Race', Diversity and nclusion'." *Race Ethnicity and Education* 17 (3): 304–325. doi:10.1080/13613324.2013.832920.

Birmingham City Council. 2007. *The Birmingham Agreed Syllabus for Religious Education*. Birmingham: Birmingham City Council.

Bonnett, A. 1997. Constructions of Whiteness in European and American Anti-racism. In *Debating Cultural Hybridity: Multi-cultural Identities and the Politics of Antiracism*, edited by P. Werbner & T. Modood, pp. 173–192. London: Zed Books

Breen, D. 2016. "'Critical Race Theory, Policy Rhetoric and Outcomes: The Case of Muslim Schools in Britain." *Race Ethnicity and Education*. http://dx.doi.org/10.1080/13613324.2016.1248828

Breen, D. 2018. *Critical Race Theory, Muslim Schools and Communities: Faith Schooling in Islamophobic Britain?* London: Palgrave-Macmillan.

Chakrabarty, N. 2012. "Buried Alive : The Psychoanalysis of Racial Absence in Preparedness/education." *Race Ethnicity and Education* 15 (1): 43-63.
Clarke, P. 2014. *Report into Allegations Concerning Birmingham Schools Arising from the 'Trojan Horse' Letter*. London: Her Majesty's Stationary Office.
Coughlan, S. 2014.. ""Disturbing" Findings from Trojan Horse Inquiry." *BBC News*, 22 July 2014, last accessed: 15/ 08/2017 http://www.bbc.co.uk/news/education-28419901
Crenshaw, K., K. Gotanda, G. Peller, and K. Thomas, Eds. 1995. *Critical Race Theory: The Key Writings that Formed the Movement*. New York: New York Press.
Delgado, R., Ed. 1995. *Critical Race Theory: The Cutting Edge*. Philadelphia: Temple University Press.
Delgado, R. 2003. "Crossroads and Blind Alleys: A Critical Examination of Recent Writing about Race." *Texas Law Review* 82: 121-152.
DfE. 1994. *Religious Education and Collective Worship*. London: Her Majesty's Stationary Office.
DfE. 2011. *Teachers' Standards Guidance for school leaders, school staff and governing bodies*. London: Crown Copyright.
DfE. 2014. *Promoting Fundamental British Values as Part of SMSC in Schools: Departmental Advice for Maintained Schools*. London: Department for Education.
DfE. 2015. *The Prevent Duty: Departmental Advice for Schools and Childcare Providers*. London: Department for Education.
Donaghy, L. 2014.. "Ofsted'S Slur on the Muslim Community of Park View School." *The Guardian*, 9 June 2014 last accessed: 15/ 08/2017 https://www.theguardian.com/commentisfree/2014/jun/09/ofsted-slur-muslim-park-view-school-values-extremism
Dudziak, M. L. 2000. *Cold War Civil Rights: Race and the Image of American Democracy*. Princeton: Princeton University Press.
Essed, P. 1991. *Understanding Everyday Racism: An Interdisciplinary Theory*. Amsterdam: University of Amsterdam.
Garner, S. 2017. "Surfing the Third Wave of Whiteness Studies: Reflections on Twine and Gallagher." *Ethnic and Racial Studies* 40 (9): 1582–1597. doi:10.1080/01419870.2017.1300301.
Gillborn, D. 2005. "Education Policy as an Act of White Supremacy: Whiteness, Critical Race Theory and Reform." *Journal of Education Policy* 20 (4): 484–505.
Gillborn, D. 2009. "Who's Afraid of Critical Race Theory in Education? a Reply to Mike Cole's 'The Color-line and The Class Struggle'." *Power and Education* 1 (1): 125-13.
Goldberg, T. G. 2006. "Racial Europeanization." *Ethnic and Racial Studies* 29 (2): 332–364.
Holmwood, J., and T. O'Toole. 2017. *Countering Extremism in British Schools? the Truth about the Birmingham Trojan Horse Affair*. Bristol: Policy Press.
Home Office. 2017. *Individuals Referred to and Supported through the Prevent Programme, April 2015 To March 2016*. London: Crown Copyright.
Housee, S. 2012. "What's The Point? Anti-racism and Students' Voices against Islamophobia." *Race Ethnicity and Education* 15 (1): 101–120.
Husband, C., and Y. Alam. 2011. *Social Cohesion and Counter-Terrorism: A Policy Contradiction?* Bristol: Policy Press.
ISC. 2017. *The 2017 Attacks: What Needs to Change? Intelligence and Security Committee of Parliament*. London: HMSO.

Ismail, S. 2017. "'East London Acid Attack: When Muslims are the Victims, We Refuse to Call It Terrorism', Independent." http://www.independent.co.uk/voices/east-london-acid-attack-terrorism-islamophobia-a7817466.html

Jackson, R. 2015. "The Epistemological Crisis of Counterterrorism." *Critical Studies on Terrorism* 8 (1): 33–54. doi:10.1080/17539153.2015.1009762.

Kershaw, I. 2014.. *Investigation report: Trojan Horse letter – report of Ian Kershaw of Northern education for Birmingham City Council in respect of issues arising as a result of concerns raised in a letter dated 27November 2013, known as the Trojan Horse letter*

Kundnani, A. 2009. *Spooked: How Not to Prevent Violent Extremism*. London: Institute of Race Relations.

Ladson-Billings, G. 1998. "Just What Is Critical Race Theory and What's It Doing in a Nice Field like Education?" *Qualitative Studies in Education* 11 (1): 7–24. doi:10.1080/095183998236863.

Leonardo, Z. 2002. "The Souls of White Folk: Critical Pedagogy, Whiteness Studies, and Globalization Discourse" *Race Ethnicity & Education* 5 (1): 29–50.

Mackie, P. 2014.. ""Islamic Takeover Plot" in Birmingham Schools Investigated." *BBC News*, 7 March 2014, last accessed: 15/ 08/2017 http://www.bbc.co.uk/news/uk-england-birmingham-26482599

Mendick, R., G. Rayner, M. Evans, and H. Dixon. 2017.. "Security Services Missed Five Opportunities to Stop the Manchester Bomber." *The Telegraph*, 6 June 2017, accessed: 15/ 08/2017 http://www.telegraph.co.uk/news/2017/05/24/security-services-missed-five-opportunities-stop-manchester/last

Miah, S. 2017. *Muslims, Schooling and Security - Trojan Horse, Prevent and Racial Politics*. London: Palgrave Macmillan.

Nayak, A. 2011. "Geography, Race and Emotions: Social and Cultural Intersections." *Social and Cultural Geography* 12 (6): 548–562. doi:10.1080/14649365.2011.601867.

O'Toole, T. 2015. "'Prevent: From 'Hearts and Minds' to 'Muscular Liberalism'." *Public Spirit*, http://www.publicspirit.org.uk/prevent-from-hearts-and-minds-to-muscular-liberalism/

O'Toole, T., N. Meer, D. DeHanas, S. Jones, and T. Modood. 2016. "Governing through Prevent? Regulation and Contested Practice in state-Muslim Engagement." *Sociology* 50 (1): 160–177. doi:10.1177/0038038514564437.

OFSTED. 2013. *School Report: Oldknow Academy (2013)*. Manchester: Office for Standards in Education, Children's Services and Skills.

OFSTED. 2014a. *School Report: Oldknow Academy (2014)*. London: Office for Standards in Education, Children's Services and Skills.

OFSTED. 2014b. *School Report: Park View School (2014)*. London: Office for Standards in Education, Children's Services and Skills.

OFSTED. 2015.. The Common Inspection Framework: Education, Skills and Early Years. Office for Standards in Education, Children's Services and Skills, London: Crown Copyright.

OSJI. 2016. *Eroding Trust: The UK's PREVENT Counter- Extremism Strategy in Health and Education*, Open Society Justice Initiative, New York: Open Society Justice Foundations.

Preston, J., and C. Chadderton. 2012. "Rediscovering 'Race Traitor': Towards a Critical Race Theory Informed Public Pedagogy." *Race, Ethnicity and Education* 15 (1): 85–100. doi:10.1080/13613324.2012.638866.

Prevent 2015. *Revised Prevent Duty Guidance: For England and Wales: Guidance for Specified Authorities in England and Wales on the Duty in the Counter-Terrorism and*

Security Act 2015 to have due Regard to the Need to Prevent People from Being Drawn into Terrorism. London: Crown Copyright.

Prevent. 2011. *Prevent Strategy*. London: HMSO.

PVET. 2014. *Statement from Park View Educational Trust on Ofsted Reports on Park View, Golden Hillock and Nansen Schools*. Birmingham: Park View Educational Trust. 9 June 2014.

Rhodes, J. 2013. "'Remaking Whiteness in the "Postracial" UK." In *The State of Race*, edited by N. Kapoor, V. S. Kalra, and J. Rhodes, 49-71. Basingstoke: Palgrave.

Rollock, N. 2012. "The Invisibility of Race: Intersectional Reflections on the Liminal Space of Alterity." *Race Ethnicity & Education* 15 (1): 65-84.

Wintour, P. 2014.. "Michael Gove Wants "British Values" on School Curriculums." *The Guardian*, 9 June 2014, https://www.theguardian.com/education/2014/jun/09/michael-gove-british-values-curriculum

Looking as white: anti-racism apps, appearance and racialized embodiment

Alana Lentin

ABSTRACT
Smartphone apps for anti-racism education and intervention are being developed by organisations in various countries. The ubiquity of smartphone use and app methodology as Grant argues, have the potential to disrupt racial knowledges and facilitate anti-racist action. I use Nicholas Mirzoeff's 'zones of appearance and non-appearance' and Derek Hook's discussion of 'racialising embodiment' to discuss the potential of one such app, Everyday Racism, to challenge and disrupt white supremacy. The Australian-based app uses gamification to encourage users to participate in 'bystander anti-racism'. However, by failing to question the neutrality of the default white bystander, the app risks reproducing hegemonic constellations of white agency versus racialized inaction. I argue that, in the zone of appearance, it is not enough to make racism apparent. It is necessary to appear. To appear first requires exposing nonappearance including the role even of the well-intentioned in maintaining it.

To be white is simply to be allowed to act.'

Nicholas Mirzoeff (2017, 24).

Introduction: spaces of appearance and nonappearance

#WeSeeYou –
(Twitter hashtag)

In his opening to *The Appearance of Black Lives Matter*, Nicholas Mirzoeff explains his use of the word 'appearance':

> To appear is to matter, in the sense of Black Lives Matter, to be grievable, to be a person that counts for something. And it is to claim the right to look, in the

sense that I see you and you see me, and together we decide what there is to say as a result. It's about seeing what there is to be seen, in defiance of the police who say "move on, there's nothing to see here," and then giving the visible a sayable name. (Mirzoeff 2017, 18)

The Twitter hashtag, #WeSeeYou is used in a variety of ways. It can signal recognition among people facing a common struggle. It can signal appreciation – we recognize your efforts on our behalf. It can also signal reprimand – we see what you are doing and we are calling you out for it. In the realm of anti-racism, the act of seeing is tied to the importance placed on making visible. As David Goldberg has written, visibility has historically been tied to whiteness (Goldberg 1997). Racism renders the racialized invisible. Harm done against those marked by race often literally goes unnoticed, is minimized or relativized even if it is physically seen. Thus, in the wake of the killing of the antifascist protestor, Heather Heyer by white supremacist James Fields in Charlottesville Virginia in August 2017, some contrasted the reception of her murder with those of Black women in the US. Social media commentator, Son of Baldwin, noted for example,

> If it was a down-ass black woman who was destroyed by a terrorist dreaming of a white world, who would rally? Who would honour? Who would grieve? […] Who would say her name? […] Who would, instead, ignore? Blame her for her own death? Search for her criminal record? Blame her parents? Blame her culture? Downplay her intelligence? […] Dare not speak her name?[1]

And although he was roundly criticized for failing to contribute to anti-racist solidarity building, the cousin of Heather Heyer, Diana Ratcliffe wrote in a similar vein,

> Why is it that the death of a white woman at the hands of a white supremacist group has finally gotten the attention of white folk? Why have we been turning our heads the other way for so long? How many black families, Latino families, Asian families, Native-American families before us have been left broken from this ugly vein of hatred in our country? (Ratcliff 2017)

The quest for visibility, therefore, is two-edged. While visibility is always a minimum condition for representation to take place, it appears insufficient if it merely causes us to see without being accompanied by self-determination (Lentin 2004). In the age of networked digital media and its pervasion into all spheres of life, this entails being in control of the images that are streamed daily across our 'feeds' (Orgad 2012). We are feeding off images of racialized violence that in turn feed the platforms we rely on for sustenance (Titley 2016). The spread of photographs and videos of police shootings of Black women and men in the US, Aboriginal children and adults in Australian jails, Muslim women attacked for wearing hijab, and endlessly on, is afforded by the existence of media infrastructures which do not exist outside of the white supremacist context in which they emerge. As Safiya Noble notes, in relation to the reception of the killing of Trayvon Martin which sparked the Black Lives Matter movement, were it not for the creative representations of the case spread across the internet, it would simply not have been given the attention it deserved. Nevertheless, it is vital to understand that 'the creation of news segments dedicated to this story, can, and often do, support dominant power structures' (Noble 2014, 14). While counternarratives are constantly developed against this, making visible is not a sufficient prerequisite for change to the system that both produces and reproduces 'state-sanctioned or state-justified forms of violence on black life' (ibid.).

For Courtney Baker, there is an important distinction to be drawn between the look and the gaze. While the gaze is dangerous and debilitating for its objects, 'not all looks are gazes' (Baker 2015, 2). Because it is what Baker calls more flexible and variegated than the gaze, the look 'has by turns been accused of violence and aligned with bravery' (ibid.). 'Learning from looking', she says, can and has been used to counter injustice (ibid.), but it does not necessarily lead to such an end. Baker observes the use of the historical representation of Black pain, in the struggle to abolish slavery or combat lynching, for example. This kind of looking, which she calls 'humane insight', appeals to onlookers' ethics through 'the spectacle of others' embodied suffering' (ibid. 5). She argues that although there is significant cost involved in 'displaying black bodies in states of ruin', there is evidence that the aim of this display is ultimately a concern with 'black humanity' (ibid.).

Chauncey Devega makes a case, in apparent contrast to Baker, for not watching the killing of Alton Sterling, tasered and fatally shot by Baton Rouge police in July 2016. The widely circulated images and videos of police murders of Black people in the US are, he writes, 'the contemporary version of lynching culture in the digital age' (DeVega 2016). However, while Devega proposes that these images are 'psychologically and spiritually unhealthy for black Americans', he does not want everyone to turn away. Watching the footage of these killings can serve as 'an antidote against white denial, white lies' in the United States (ibid.). However, he warns that 'there are likely a good number of white Americans who are titillated by video recordings of police violence against people of colour' (ibid.). Indeed, LeRon Barton has written that, for him, 'watching Black men being beaten on video is the new lynching postcard' (Barton 2017). And contra Baker, he argues that the existence of this footage does not act as necessary proof because it is untrue to say that 'whites are ignorant about racism' (ibid.).

Nevertheless, Mirzoeff argues forcefully for Black Lives Matter, the movement that began as a hashtag instigated by three Black Queer women – Alicia Garza, Patrisse Cullors, and Opal Tometi – as a 'space of appearance' that resists representation. Representation necessarily excludes and limits what is present in the quest to create an image. Appearance, in contrast, resists the hierarchies and exclusions of the politics of recognition. For Mirzoeff, in the space of appearance, those who show up see each other 'and a space is formed by that exchange' (Mirzoeff 2017, 32). He suggests that, in this space, which 'does not end racial hierarchy', nevertheless, a vision of a potential, abolitionist, future in common can be imaged. The 'space of appearance' in which the importance of Black lives is performed (the space of appearance 'does not represent, it performs': 33) is both actual and potential. The potential is captured through visual documentation. However, many of these photographs and videos are unable to capture the 'refusal and resistance' because they are mediated by power. Who takes a photograph and to which end is not insignificant. For example, Ramsey Orta was jailed for four years after filming the police murder of Eric Garner in 2014. Police photographs and videos, in contrast, look 'how the state wants its subject to look, not how people see themselves' (ibid. 34).

In Mirzoeff's analysis of the trial of Darren Wilson, accused and ultimately acquitted of shooting the Black teenager, Michael Brown, he makes use of the archive of 'supplementary witness statements, interview transcripts, forensic reports, media clips, and photographs'. These materials reveal the 'entire apparatus of social control' which the police enact but which remain untransparent to the majority of the population (ibid. 137). What becomes clear is, that the presentation of materials alongside selective interpretations of events and against a backdrop of pre-determining racialized 'knowledge' about Black people and the police serve to present a distorted picture of the event which refutes witness accounts. To counter this, Mirzoeff's visual analysis involves editing still images of scenes of police shootings of Black people in the US to 'exclude the fallen or about-to-be-wounded person' (ibid. 119). He explains that doing this brings into focus the 'spaces of nonappearance' in which these fatal incidents overwhelmingly occur: 'the "nonplaces" of consumer society' (ibid. 118). By giving primacy to the scenes in which murders take place, rather than focusing the look on the victim, Mirzoeff is able to emphasise the context that is usually ignored or taken for granted; the 'spaces of nonappearance' that he calls America': 'an ideology, not a geography, the militarized white supremacy of the settler colony' (ibid. 119).

Mirzoeff's spaces of nonappearance are the spaces of whiteness. While his work specifies the context of the US, both the historical parallels between it and other settler colonial societies, and the global media landscape in which Black Lives Matter appears and has an impact, suggest the utility of 'nonappearance' as a concept beyond the US. In our critical times, racism and white supremacy circulate with ease in the borderless landscapes of digital media (Sharma 2013), aided in large part by the growth and spread of mobile technologies. So, in (re)imagining the potential futures of anti-racism, what analytical role is to be played by appearance and nonappearance? If the 'space of appearance' is a potential – a space 'that doesn't reproduce white supremacy', then what can anti-racism do to bring this about, especially at a time when Mirzoeff correctly states, 'significant minorities of whites [...] no longer accept the antiracist formation of the social' (ibid. 180)? While the need for action to be taken to confront racism at both systemic and interpersonal levels is vital (Nelson, Dunn, and Paradies 2011), questions need to be asked about how the spaces in which this action takes place are represented. In other words, how may anti-racism initiatives, especially those that involve visual representations as is increasingly common with the widespread use of digital communications, inadvertently participate in zoning out the 'spaces of nonappearance'?

To examine this question, I discuss research I carried out on five anti-racism apps developed by organisations in Australia, France, and the UK. After discussing the main findings of the research, I analyse one app in particular, the 'Everyday Racism' mobile app, developed by Australian anti-racism charity, *Altogether Now*, a pedagogical tool to encourage 'bystander antiracism'. I argue that the app design creates an altered space of appearance by editing out the role played by those targeted by racism in unveiling the 'spaces of *non*appearance'. As Mirzoeff, Baker, as well as Simone Browne in her discussion of the importance of 'sousveillance' as a retaliatory tool used by enslaved Black people against white oppression all show (Browne 2015), it is those targeted by racism who reveal the operations of white supremacy at play in scenarios that are often presented as 'isolated events' in dominant accounts (Lentin 2016). The Everyday Racism app, by prioritising the white gaze but obscuring the potential role played by white players of the game in perpetuating the 'spaces of nonappearance', runs the risk of damaging the potential for anti-racism to participate in unveiling rather than concealing the workings of whiteness. It presents the experience of racism as something to be consumed and reacted to, rather than as something that we all have a stake in reproducing. I use Derek Hook's discussion of 'racialising embodiment' to further argue that racialized people are presented as embodied in the digital schema of the Everyday Racism app while, in contrast, white consumers of their experiences remain disembodied, and thus unmarked by race/whiteness (Hook 2008). How may the interventions of white actors in these spaces serve to reconstitute these spaces as neutral ones that can be altered by their actions as well-intentioned agents while simultaneously avoiding to address their investment in the spaces of nonappearance?

Mobile anti-racisms

Research into race, digital technology and the Internet (Nakamura 2007; Daniels 2009, 2011, 2013; Sharma 2013; Titley 2014) stresses that the digital both changes our understandings of race and creates new types of racial inequality (Nakamura and Chow-White 2012). Despite the ubiquitous use of mobile smartphones, there has been little research carried out as yet into the ways in which they may produce and reproduce racial understandings of the social world. This seems strange considering the recent uptake of app technology as a tool for potentially combatting racism. As Grant points out, the everydayness of digital apps as they are delivered, apparently seamlessly, through the touch-screen at our fingertips, means it is an interesting methodology for thinking about anti-racist responses (Grant 2014). For Grant, apps may be particularly successful tools for responding to racism for a number of reasons: Apps intervene by 'pushing' data to us and forcing a response, they interrupt and 'colonise' time, they are continually updated, thus having the capacity to be responsive to racism's context and time, as well as its chameleonic nature.

> Furthermore, apps are multidisciplinary, using visual, discursive, geographical, historical, symbolic and social understandings and knowledges to both attract and keep their user base. Apps rely on mixed media, such as video, image stills and audio components, to create meaningful and interesting interactions with the user's environment. (Grant 2014, 24)

Grant's discussion of apps as an anti-racism methodology reveals their potential power. She notes four specific ways in which apps can act as transformative anti-racist tools, through flagging, showing the organisation of space, including excluded narratives, and mitigating consequences. Digital flagging, for example through the use of push notifications, can alert us to an otherwise unnoticed situation. An example of this is the 'Welcome to Country app' developed in Australia by Werianna Street Media.[2] Using notifications, the app alerts the user when s/he is crossing into the country of a different Aboriginal people. By responding to the notification, one can learn about the history and customs of the country and its people. This app also works to reveal the organisation of space. As Grant notes, 'I am not, for instance, continually reminded of the racialized histories and excluded peoples and their stories in the spaces I regularly inhabit' (ibid. 26). The 'Welcome to Country' app can discomfit white visions of the landscape she inhabits and thinks of as 'hers' by reminding her that it continues to be colonised and that its 'everydayness' is built on top of 80,000 years of Aboriginal presence.

Researching anti-racism apps

Despite the potentials Grant outlines, the study I co-led demonstrated that the very utility of app technology – its existence on a personal device with which we have a more and more intimate relationship (Cumiskey and Hjorth 2013) – is what potentially stops it becoming a fully effective anti-racism tool (Lentin and Humphry 2016). Our research into the use of anti-racism apps for intervention and education in five apps developed in the UK, France and Australia revealed that all five gave priority to individualised responses to racism. As a result, racism is represented as an incident or an 'act', an everyday event, which can be responded to by a person with the aid of technology. While these apps are well disposed to exposing and manifesting isolated incidents of racism in everyday life, they run the risk of playing down systemic racism and its consequences while prioritising individuals as both victims and challengers. In the terms set out by Mirzoeff, they possibly contribute to 'editing' the zone of nonappearance in ways that frame out its structural whiteness. Anti-racism is thus rewritten as something that is in the control of the individual actor whose access to mobile phone technology allows her to both consume racist disadvantage as digitally delivered spectacle and to perform anti-racist opposition and diffuse her actions via the same device. What this means for the creation of mutually co-constitutive zones of appearance in which the individual appears only insofar as she has submitted to a process in which a collective response is elaborated will be discussed in the conclusion.

Nuancing the critique of the apps' individualised focus, our study identified two types of apps, the first of which has greater potential to go beyond this. This type was community-based and focused on capturing, reporting and responding to racist incidents and/or making certain forms of racism visible, in particular, Islamophobia. A second type emphasised challenging racism through raising awareness and encouraging individuals/bystanders (who are themselves not usually the subject of racist attacks and harassment) to oppose it. A third form of antiracism app has since become increasingly available, mainly in the United States and Canada, as a tool for recording and diffusing incidents of police violence. Apps such as 'Copwatch' and 'Copblock' or the ACLU 'Stop and Frisk' app[3] are increasingly being promoted as powerful tools of 'sousveillance' (Browne 2015), complementing the autonomous documentation of violence that has accompanied the proliferation of Black Lives Matter as both a movement and an archive of evidence. However, they have not as yet been the object of scholarly research; a further stage of our project seeks to look at the potential of these apps to play a role both in revealing the structuring effects of race, and contributing to a future freedom that the 'zone of appearance' seeks for all.

The community-based apps we examined were both developed to combat Islamophobia. In fact, the Australian 'Islamophobia Watch' app was modelled in part on the French 'Appli CCIF', a tool released by the French anti-Islamophobia organisation, the CCIF. Both apps allowed users to report incidents of Islamophobic racism and build up a picture of Islamophobic incidents in each country that then serves to grow awareness of the frequency and severity of Islamophobia. In the French case, this was stressed by the organisation's spokesperson as vital. The app may not be the first port of call for those wishing to report an incident of Islamophobia, given that it is also possible to do so via phone or the

CCIF website. Therefore, the organisation's end goal is to raise awareness of the existence of Islamophobia, a contested category of racism in contemporary France. It is through the app's additional function, as a news feed, that it achieves this. Users can add news items about Islamophobia to the app that then go through a vetting process. In our interview with CCIF, its spokesperson said that this creates a bottom-up 'citizen journalism' that serves as a counterweight to 'the official channels for relaying information' (Lentin and Humphry 2016).

In that the forum-based function of the newsfeed encourages community participation so that users become co-creators of the app's contents, the 'Appli du CCIF' goes beyond the merely individual level. Nevertheless, the majority of users ('the app is used a great deal, we're at 1500 – about 1500 – views per screen everyday') consume its contents more passively. The organisation reported that it was mainly used as a news source scrolled through while riding the Metro, etc.. Other apps, 'Islamophobia Watch' and a second French app, the veteran anti-racism organization *La Licra's* 'Citoyens Effaçons le racisme', were less widely used. A second stage of our study will examine usage and usability data in greater detail. However, an interview with the *Licra* representatives revealed that, although the app had been downloaded 7–8,000 times, it was not often used to report the incidents of racist graffiti that it was set up to. Our interview revealed that the organisation is disappointed with what was seen as a failure of the app to lead to more recruitment to the cause: '…we don't recruit many people. So we have to improve what we do'.

Unlike the CCIF whose mainly community-oriented interface has the capacity to build resistance to Islamophobia from among Muslim users, the 'Citoyens Effaçons le racisme' app suffers from an additional problem that, beyond individualisation, goes more deeply towards explaining the problems that several of the apps we looked at have in challenging the spaces of whiteness/nonappearance in which racism takes effect. The *Licra*, like other so-called 'majoritarian' antiracist organisations in France, are strongly committed to a universalist vision of anti-racism (Lentin 2004). Under this view, not only are racialized groups not considered to be the primary agents of anti-racism – 'we must open out to the general public' (*Licra*) – but racism itself can be enacted by anyone. The *Licra* thus agrees that 'anti-white' racism exists. Indeed, it supported the efforts by Paris Mayor, Anne Hidalgo, to have the Nyansapo Afro-feminist conference in Paris in July 2017 cancelled because it planned to have certain spaces reserved for Black and racialized women which she saw as discriminatory and exclusionary (AFP 2017). In a perfect example of how the histories of anti-racism, anticolonialism and the civil rights movement have sometimes been co-opted in the service of race-blind universalism, the *Licra* representative said of the festival, 'Rosa Parks must be turning in her grave'.[4] This earned it the commendation of far-right group, *Français de souche* which tweeted, 'thanks to Anne Hidalgo and the LICRA for relaying Francais de Souche's message and taking action [against the conference]'.[5]

There appears, therefore, to be a link between the political context in which the Licra operates, widely criticised by autonomous and 'decolonial' anti-racist groups, such as the *Mouvement des indigènes de la république* (MIR), *Les Indivisibles*, the CCIF, or *The Anti-Negrophobia Brigade*, and the uptake of the app they developed, which the organisation admits has not met its aim of being a tool for recruitment (Liminana Dembélé 2016). This points to the fact that problems with anti-racism apps specifically do not exist outside the wider questions with which anti-racism has always had to contend: can anti-racism ever be colour-blind? Against a backdrop of debates about what form the fight against overt white supremacy as well as ongoing state racism should take, this question is increasingly urgent. As mobile app technology becomes more and more a part of the anti-racism toolkit, it is important we ask, can these tools participate in challenging whiteness/the spaces of nonappearance or are there ways in which both their functionality and their underlying philosophies participate in compounding it?

Embodying racism and anti-racism

Whether an app was community based or had the wider remit of encouraging participation in anti-racism action, as in the case of the *Licra* app or 'Kick it Out', an app for reporting racism on British football terraces, had an impact on the extent to which it could be said to have a transformative effect for groups and individuals affected by racism. While four of the apps were focused on reporting racist incidents and differed only in terms of which groups had developed them and what their underlying philosophy was, a fifth app had an entirely different orientation. The Australian 'Everyday Racism' app, developed by antiracism charity *Altogether Now*, is a pedagogical tool. Interviewed for the study, *Altogether Now*'s director claimed the app was developed to teach users about antiracism, 'encouraging them to learn over a period of time about what they could do'. The app was conceived for 'the bystander', who has not necessarily experienced first-hand what it is like to be the target of racism. It uses gamification to increase users' understanding of racism by 'walking in someone's shoes' (Everyday Racism appstore promotional material). Users select one of three characters to 'be' while playing the game: an Aboriginal man, a Muslim woman and an Indian student. There is a final option of playing as 'Yourself' (see Figure 1). The game is played over a seven-day period during which the player receives a range of alerts, tweets, videos, and images of situations of 'everyday racism' experienced by one of the three racialized characters, or if playing as 'yourself', witnessed by you. It thus meets Grant's methodological criteria in several ways: the app 'pushes' data to us eliciting a response, it interrupts time, and has the potential to be continually updated. Nevertheless, there are several problems with the app philosophy and design which raise concerns as to its ability to effectively subvert the 'zone of nonapperance'.

Approaching the 'Everyday Racism' app from within a perspective on gaming, Fordyce, Neale, and Apperley (2016) identify some of the key elements which I wish to problematise here. Their criticism focuses on the fourth character, 'Yourself'. Yourself is presented as a 'neutral' silhouette. Hence, 'this figure,

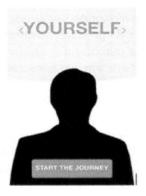

Figure 1. Everyday racism app publicity materials.

in being unmarked, is the implicit white norm a case which is reinforced as the player experiences other positions ...' (Fordyce, Neale, and Apperley 2016, 12).

They query the fact that 'Yourself', unlike the game's other characters, remains invisible and never experiences racism. Rather, 'The unmarked "You" is always a third party to racialized abuse' (ibid.). Therefore, although, in principle 'Yourself' can be played by anyone who downloads the app, the combination of the avatar's racelessness and the fact that they never experience racism leaves no doubt that 'Yourself' is intended to embody whiteness. Nevertheless, the choice of characters was made through consultation with a reference committee made up of Aboriginal, Muslim and Indian members. From this the everyday scenarios used in the app programming were gathered with developers testing a range of scenarios with the group over several weeks. The presumed neutrality of 'Yourself' was, however, not questioned by the developers in this process. The option to play as 'yourself' runs the risk of entrenching a view of the anti-racist actor as a raceless (and genderless) figure, a universalised actor whose central location in the potential 'space of appearance' in which anti-racist futures have the potential to be speculatively explored through play configures it as one in which whiteness goes untroubled. We should thus ask whether the Everyday Racism app has the potential to go beyond colour-blind visions of anti-racism. Given that a second version of the app has been developed for school children[6] this is particularly urgent, schools being a key site for the reproduction of racism (Mansouri and Jenkins 2010) and whiteness (Castagno 2014).

Bystander anti-racism

In order to further explore this question, it is necessary to set the app in context by discussing its remit of encouraging 'bystander anti-racism'. *Altogether Now* collaborated with researchers involved in the 'Challenging Racism' project, a large-scale government funded research project by academics from a number of Australian universities focused on measuring societal attitudes to racism and encouraging popular responses to it. The concept of 'bystander anti-racism' has been elaborated on by Nelson, Dunn, and Paradies (2011) all of whom are investigators on the 'Challenging Racism' project. Bystander anti-racism aims 'to stop the perpetration of racism, reduce its escalation, prevent the physical, psychological, and social harms that may result, and/or strengthen broader social norms that should reduce racism in the future' (ibid. 265). One of the main benefits of the bystander approach, according to the authors, is that it constructs 'racist acts as a deviance' (ibid. 280). However, as I have noted elsewhere (Lentin 2017), by privileging an individualised response in which racism is construed as aberrant rather than systemic, and the emphasis is placed on racism in public (Lentin 2016), the bystander approach largely displaces race while appearing to challenge racism. In particular, by failing to problematise the centrality given to heroic bystanders in events of racism framed as isolated incidents, it is problematic as a tool for challenging whiteness/the zone of nonappearance.

The Everyday Racism app, although autonomous, sits within a digital ecology of 'bystander anti-racism'. In Australia, much attention has been placed on incidents of racism, especially on public transport, due to a perceived increase in attacks mainly due to the possibility of recording them using smartphones and diffusing the footage online (Lentin 2016). On its opening page, the Challenging Racism website asks, 'Did you know that almost 40% of racist incidents occur in public spaces, including on public transport?' (Challenging Racism, Website). In response, the project produced four bystander anti-racism videos (ibid.). Elsewhere I have discussed the potential for these videos to inadvertently anchor rather than displace whiteness (Lentin 2017). Most notably, the combined centring of white bystanders who intervene in racist scenarios in each of the videos, along with the presentation of those enacting the racism as of mixed ethnicities raises questions about how racism and anti-racism are defined and embodied. This question is of particular importance given the ongoing Anglo colonisation of Aboriginal lands in what is today known as Australia.

'Everyday racism' and the embodiment of whiteness

The 'Everyday Racism' app participates in the establishment of bystander anti-racism as above all a white endeavour. Both the app and the videos construct white people as having the potential to take action against racism while neither being named as the perpetrators of racism or as the beneficiaries of whiteness within a context of Anglo-Australian dominance (Laforteza 2016, Moreton-Robinson 2015). The app in particular, by failing to embody the player, 'Yourself', presents the possibility of neutrality in relation to race as self-evident. The app allows for three categories of people: those who are raced (racialized minorities in need of protection), those who are racist and have agency (the problem to be countered), and those who are non- or anti-racist, represented by a raceless silhouette, who, as potential bystanders, also have agency.[7]

Hook's discussion of Chabani Manganyi and Frantz Fanon's theorisations of 'racialising embodiment' is useful in thinking through the problems in the way the Everyday Racism app presents these raced and race-neutral characters in the two-fold aim of making racism visible and encouraging those with an agency to take action (Hook 2008). For the South African psychoanalyst, Manganyi, the most persistent equation in western culture is that of whiteness with the mind and blackness with the body; the former being seen as superior to the latter (Manganyi 1981). This dichotomy is evident in the choice made by the app designers to represent 'Yourself' as disembodied and thus, raceless. Racelessness is equated with whiteness and thus cerebral and, in the context of the app's intent – to provoke bystander anti-racism action – is presented as capable of stepping back from and conceptualising racism in order to take action. In contrast, the raced characters are embodied, and as Manganyi says, in the racial schema, 'devalued, deserving of denial and repression' and, in this context, also perhaps of pity (Hook 2008, 144).

The Everyday Racism app, built for use in a (settler) colonial country, presents the embodiment of racism as a problem to be solved via the three racialised characters, Aisha, Vihaan, and Patrick. In the context of colonial racial rule with which Hook, via Manganyi and Fanon, is interested, 'the balance of the body's relation to the world, to other bodies, to its own positive identity, to an array of cultural and historical values, is almost completely obliterated' (ibid. 148). The result of this is evoked by Fanon when he describes his perception of his own Blackness as 'crushing objecthood' (Fanon 2008, 82), or the inability to separate the self from 'the "psycho-materiality" of objects animated by racist beliefs' (Hook 2008, 148). This leads, to an intersection of 'two traumatic conditions... "embodied absence" and "disembodied presence"' (ibid.). Hook explains that, for Fanon, this double trauma means that he 'experiences his physical being in a series of mutilated disjunctions' (ibid.). Embodied absence refers to souls 'evacuated of psychological presence' (ibid.). In the app, the experiences of

Aisha, Vihaan and Patrick are consumed as alerts and texts sent to the player of the game, but no insight into their psychic state is offered and their viewpoints are not presented. Neither are their opinions about how to counter the racism they are facing sought. They therefore have no possibility to act upon the structures of racism. They are there but not there.

In contrast, disembodied presence symbolises whiteness. Fanon is made hyper aware of his Black body as it is thrown against the backdrop filled with the 'insignias of disembodied whiteness' (ibid. 147): the 'space of nonappearance'. Whiteness literally does not need to be represented in the body because it is the 'white song' evoked by Fanon, the theme music to his bodily existence in the colonial world. In 'Everyday Racism', this white context is represented by 'Yourself'. Only 'Yourself', can be the true knower of racism because its purported racelessness frees it from the dual trauma that embodied absence/disembodied presence elicits in those presented as 'having race', as opposed to being racially unmarked. The Everyday racism app, by embodying the raced characters and disembodying 'Yourself', attributes the power to define racism to those unaffected by it whose neutrality affords them objectivity and, it is suggested, is what empowers them to act.

Drawing on Fanon's descriptions of epidermalisation, Hook argues that understanding racism requires understanding how race and racism get 'under the skin' so that what he calls, 'objectified souls' are spliced with 'subjectified objects' (Hook 2008, 148). Reaching into grasp how racism feels, it is suggested, must begin with the lived experience of racism that the Everyday racism app transmits. But it also necessitates a 'real dialectical interchange' (ibid.). The disembodied presence of 'Yourself' and the player's role as a consumer of racist experiences, whose own investment in the maintenance of white structures is obscured, destabilises the basis upon which such an interchange could take place. Only the experiences of the racialized characters are brought 'to the table' while both the unraced, white 'Yourself' and those who play at being Aisha, Patrick or Vihaan do not have to unveil themselves, maintaining a cerebral, disembodied presence represented by the unmarked avatar and the anonymous player. In short, the structural context of white supremacy, or what Mirzoeff calls the 'space of nonappearance', is not given a face or a body thus allowing 'Yourself' to preserve 'white innocence' (Wekker 2016). This position is further entrenched by the player's claim to a moral stance in that s/he has chosen to participate in anti-racist pedagogy by downloading and playing the Everyday Racism app.

Conclusion

As described in the introduction, as we become accustomed to living in and through digital space, we are continually confronted with visual representations, including all forms of racial and racist data from the banal to the extremely violent (Sharma 2013, 2016). It is fitting that, in response, anti-racists attempt to harness the technological tools that are under constant development to challenge and overturn what is often presented as growing amounts of racism at interpersonal and societal levels. Apps such as those for reporting and recording racist incidents may be criticised for presenting individualised rather than collective responses to racism. However, in that they are a part of a larger toolkit, it is arguable that apps such as Islamophobia Watch or Copwatch have the capacity for complementing an already existing anti-racist ecology, although this necessitates further study.

In contrast, the Everyday Racism app, despite having the aim of bringing racism to the attention of those for whom the extent of racist abuse may remain unknown, risks reproducing the gaze that, Baker warns, debilitates those in its sights. Looking as opposed to gazing necessitates reciprocity or, as Mirzoeff puts it in this discussion of the transformative potential of the zone of appearance, 'I see you and you see me, and together we decide what there is to say' (Mirzoeff 2017, 18). Because Everyday Racism focuses on making racism visible, it may contribute to consciousness raising and empathy building. However, the app fails to elicit questions as to what underlies the fact that anti-racism is no longer accepted by 'significant minorities of whites' (Mirzoeff 2017, 180). Is it just that those not affected by racism need to be convinced that it is a real phenomenon? Or is it, as LeRon Barton says, untrue to say that whites are ignorant? Making visible appears insufficient unless accompanied by the ability of those affected by racism to direct the course of action. For example, perhaps bystander reactions are not always wanted, as some argued in the wake of the anti-Islamophobia #IllRideWithYou hashtag in Australia (Bahrawi 2014)? Moreover, the apparently pressing need to enlighten whites about racism circumvents the fact that the circulation of racist events through the Internet and social media into news media and back drives a cycle of intensive visibility that can be both mobilising, but also risks a neglect of the 'ambient racism' that Sharma reminds us underscores and penetrates our digital lives in potentially disabling ways (Sharma 2016).

In the zone of appearance, it is not enough to make racism apparent. It is necessary to appear. To appear first requires exposing nonappearance including the role even of the well-intentioned in maintaining it. The question remains, is it possible to conceive of technologies that produce the connective formations that can overcome both the individualisation of the mobile app form and the restrictive optics that embodiment/disembodiment produce? As effective challenges to the 'oppressive and false' nature of white supremacy (Roediger 1994, 13) the potential of anti-racism apps remains to be seen.

Disclosure statement

No potential conflict of interest was reported by the author.

Notes

1. Son of Baldwin Facebook Page. 15 August 2017.https://www.facebook.com/sonofbaldwinfb/?hc_ref=ARQFRN0oGM1ut_Rzu5HD5JVVXIMK1vcT4cXC0XGsmnwNHJifElp8rEQ1ZtlTzbCJppU&fref=nf. Accessed 17 August 2017.
2. Welcome to Country app. http://welcometocountry.mobi. Accessed 8 September 2017.
3. 'Copwatch' app: https://itunes.apple.com/us/app/cop-watch-video-recorder/id757572626?mt=8. 'Copblock' app: https://www.copblock.org/apps/. ACLU 'Stop and Frisk' app. https://www.aclu.org/blog/mass-incarceration/stop-and-frisk-watch-keep-tabs-nypd-your-smart-phone. Accessed 8 September 2017.
4. LICRA Twitter account. https://twitter.com/_licra_/status/868123586518757376?lang=en. Accessed 7 September 2017.
5. *Français de souche* website. http://www.fdesouche.com/856259-un-festival-avec-des-espaces-interdits-aux-blancs-organise-cet-ete#. Accessed 7 September 2017.
6. Altogether Now website. http://alltogethernow.org.au/app-for-children/ Accessed 7 September 2017.
7. The simple binary of agentic neutral/white versus agency-less racialized is problematised of course in the Challenging Racism bystander anti-racism videos because the racist perpetrators are always portrayed as being of diverse ethnicities. I am also mindful of Weheliye's important criticism of agency and resistance as necessary markers of freedom whose Eurocentric frame blind us 'to the manifold occurrences of freedom in zones of indistinction' (Weheliye 2014, 2). He asks what freedoms we would be alert to if resistance and agency were not the main lens through which we adjudicate whether groups or individuals are involved in acts, however small, of liberation. He echoes the 1974 Black feminist Combahee River Statement which reminded, 'if Black women were free, it would mean that everyone else would have to be free since our freedom would necessitate the destruction of all the systems of oppression' (Combahee River Collective 1974). In other words, the direction of flow is from the bottom up rather than, as suggested by 'Everyday Racism' from top-down.

ORCID

Alana Lentin http://orcid.org/0000-0001-8946-4853

References

AFP. 2017. "Paris Mayor Demands Black Feminist Festival that 'Prohibits' White People Be Banned." *The Guardian*. May 28. Accessed 5 September 2017. https://www.theguardian.com/world/2017/may/29/paris-mayor-demands-black-feminist-festival-prohibits-white-people-banned-nyansapo

Bahrawi, N. 2014. "Why #illridewithyou is an ill ride." *Al Jazeera*. Accessed September 9 2017. http://www.aljazeera.com/indepth/opinion/2014/12/why-illridewithyou-an-ill-ride-2014121712402325335.html

Baker, C. 2015. *Humane Insight: Looking at Images of African American Suffering and Death*. Chicago: University of Illinois Press.

Barton, L. 2017. "Stop Sharing Black Pain." *The Good Men Project*, August 17. Accessed 31 August 2017. https://goodmenproject.com/featured-content/stop-sharing-black-pain-wcz/

Browne, S. 2015. *Dark Matters: On the Surveillance of Blackness*. Durham NC: Duke UP.

Castagno, A. E. 2014. *Educated in Whiteness: Good Intentions and Diversity in Schools*. Minneapolis, MN: University of Minnesota Press.

Challenging Racism. "Website." Accessed February 4 2016. http://www.uws.edu.au/school-of-social-sciences-and-psychology/ssap/research/challenging_racism and https://www.westernsydney.edu.au/challengingracism/challenging_racism_project/our_research/bystander_anti-racism

Combahee River Collective. 1974. "The Combahee River Collective Statement." Accessed September 7 2017. http://americanstudies.yale.edu/sites/default/files/files/Keyword%20Coalition_Readings.pdf

Cumiskey, K. M., and L. Hjorth. ProQuest. 2013. *Mobile Media Practices, Presence and Politics: The Challenge of Being Seamlessly Mobile*. New York: Routledge.

Daniels, J. 2009. *Cyber Racism: White Supremacy Online and the New Attack on Civil Rights*. Lanham, MD: Rowman & Littlefield.

Daniels, J. 2011. *Google Bombs, Astroturf, and Cloaked Sites: Propaganda in the Digital Era (Framing 21st Century Social Issues)*. London: Routledge.

Daniels, J. 2013. "Race and Racism in Internet Studies: A Review and Critique." *New Media & Society* 15 (5): 695–719. doi:10.1177/1461444812462849.

DeVega, C. 2016. "A Modern Day Lynching: Why I Will Not Watch the Video of Alton Sterling Being Killed by Baton Rouge Police." *Salon*, July 7. Accessed 5 September 2017. http://www.salon.com/2016/07/07/a_modern_day_lynching_why_i_will_not_watch_the_video_of_alton_sterling_being_killed_by_baton_rouge_police/

Fanon, F. 2008. *Black Skin, White Masks*. London: Pluto Press.

Fordyce, R., T. Neale, and T. Apperley. 2016. "Modelling Systemic Racism: Mobilising the Dynamics of Race and Games in Everyday Racism." *The FibreCulture Journal* 27: FCJ–200.

Goldberg, D. T. 1997. *Racial Subjects: Writing on Race in America*. New York and London: Routledge.

Grant, N. E. 2014. "The Antiracism App: Methodological Reflections for Theory and Practice." *Critical Literacy: Theories & Practices* 8 (1): 20–35.

Hook, D. 2008. "The "Real" of Racializing Embodiment." *Journal of Community & Applied Social Psychology* 18: 140–152. doi:10.1002/casp.963.

Laforteza, E. M. C. 2016. *The Somatechnics of Whiteness and Race: Colonialism and Mestiza Privilege*. London: Routledge.

Lentin, A. 2004. *Racism and Anti-Racism in Europe*. London: Pluto Press.

Lentin, A. 2016. "Racism in Public or Public Racism: Doing Antiracism in 'Postracial' Times." *Ethnic and Racial Studies* 39 (1): 33–48. doi:10.1080/01419870.2016.1096409.

Lentin, A. 2017. "(Not) Doing Race: The Discourse on 'Casual Racism', 'Bystander Antiracism' and 'Ordinariness' in Australian Racism Studies." In *Critical Reflections on Australian Migration Research*, edited by V. Marotta and M. Boese, 125-143. London: Routledge.

Lentin, A., and J. Humphry. 2016. "Antiracism Apps: Framing Understandings and Approaches to Antiracism Education and Intervention." *Information, Communication and Society* 20 (10): 1539–1553. doi:10.1080/1369118X.2016.1240824.

Liminana Dembélé, C. 2016. "Le racisme anti-blanc, une expression présente de la domination eurocentrée." *Mediapart*, January 29. https://blogs.mediapart.fr/cathy-liminana-dembele/blog/290116/le-racisme-anti-blanc-une-expression-presente-de-la-domination-eurccentree-1

Manganyi, N. C. 1981 *Looking through the Keyhole: Dissenting Essays on the Black Experience*. Johannesburg: Ravan Press.

Mansouri, F., and L. Jenkins. 2010. "Schools as Sites of Race Relations and Intercultural Tension." *Australian Journal of Teacher Education* 35 (7): 93–108. doi:10.14221/ajte.2010v35n7.8.

Mirzoeff, N. 2017. *The Appearance of Black Lives Matter*. Miami, FL: NAME Publications.

Moreton-Robinson, A 2015. *The White Possessive: Property, Power, and Indigenous Sovereignty*. Minneapolis, MN: University of Minnesota Press.

Nakamura, L. 2007. *Digitizing Race: Visual Cultures of the Internet*. London: University of Minnesota Press.

Nakamura, L., and P. A. Chow-White. 2012. "Introduction: Race and Digital Technology: Code, the Color Line and the Information Societies." In *Race after the Internet*, edited by L. Nakamura and P. A. Chow-White, 1-17. London: Routledge.

Nelson, J. K., K. Dunn, and Y. Paradies. 2011. "Bystander Anti-Racism: A Review of the Literature." *Analyses of Social Issues and Public Policy* 11 (1): 263–284. doi:10.1111/j.1530-2415.2011.01274.x.

Noble, S. O. 2014. "Teaching Trayvon: Race, Media, and the Politics of Spectacle." *The Black Scholar* 44 (1): 12–29. doi:10.1080/00064246.2014.11641209.

Orgad, S. 2012. *Media Representation and the Global Imagination*. London: Polity.

Ratcliff, D. 2017. "Heather Heyer's Cousin: Racism Will Get Worse unless We Stop It Now." CNN, August 20. Accessed 31 August 2017 https://amp.cnn.com/cnn/2017/08/19/opinions/heather-heyer-cousin-racism-has-no-place-in-america/index.html

Roediger, D. 1994. *Towards the Abolition of Whiteness: Essays on Race, Politics, and Working Class History*. London: Verso.

Sharma, S. 2013. "Black Twitter? Racial Hashtags, Networks and Contagion." *New Formations* 78: 46–64. doi:10.3898/NewF.78.02.2013.

Sharma, S. 2016. "Exploring Racism Denial Talk on Twitter." In *Digital Sociologies*, edited by J. Daniels, K. Gregory, and T. McMillan Cottom, 463–486. Bristol: Policy Press.

Titley, G. 2014. "No Apologies for Cross-Posting: European Trans-Media Space and the Digital Circuitries of Racism." *Crossings: Journal of Migration & Culture* 5 (1): 41-55.

Titley, G. 2016. "Or are We All Postracial Yet?" *Ethnic and Racial Studies* 39 (13): 2269–2277. doi:10.1080/01419870.2016.1202434.

Weheliye, A. 2014. *Habeas Viscus: Racializing Assemblages, Biopolitics, and Black Feminist Theories of the Human*. Durham: Duke University Press.

Wekker, G. 2016. *White Innocence: Paradoxes of Colonialism and Race*. Durham NC: Duke University Press.

Index

Note: Figures and tables are shown in *italics* and **bold** type respectively, and footnotes by "n" and the note number after the page number e.g., 128n6 refers to note number 6 on page 128.

Abedi, Salman 107, 108
acceptance, of racial segregation 85, 88–89
affirmative action 13, 65
alienation 14, 18, 96, 110
Altogether Now app 118, 122, 124, 128n6
analytical apologetics 1–2
ancestry 29, 50, 56–57
anthropology 2, 34, 36, 41, 73
anti-immigration 6, 13, 46
anti-Islamophobia 120, 127; *see also* CCIF (Collectif Contre l'Islamophobie en France)
anti-Muslim racism 30
anti-racism 1, 8, 15, 97, 120, 122; apps for 114–127, *123*; bystander 114, 118, 124, 125, 128n7
apartheid 7, 39, 40, 41, 42; and British-born South Africans 79–92
appearance 64, 114, 116–117, *117–118*, 120, *123*, 127
Appearance of Black Lives Matter, The 114–115
'Appli du CCIF' (app) 120, 121
apps, smartphone 114–127, *123*, 128n3
artistic expression 5, 63, 64, 70, 71, 72, 73, 74, 75
assimilation 51–52, 66–67, 68
austerity 16, 17, 30, 33

'banal nationalism' 31–32
Benjamin, Walter 1
Biasini, Emile 72
Black and Minority Ethnic communities 16, 17
Black Skin, White Masks 52

boundary reimagination, of racial segregation 85, 87–88
Brexit (British Exit) 7, 46, 58; and whiteness, populism and racialisation of UK and US working class 10, 11–12, 13, 14, 15, 16, 17, 18–21, *19*, **20**, **21**, 22, 23n2
British Muslims 95, 99, 105, 107, 108, 109–110
British values 96, 98–108
British-born South Africans 79–92
Bush Jr., George 20, **20**, **21**
'bystander anti-racism' 114, 118, 124, 125, 128n7

CCIF (*Collectif Contre l'Islamophobie en France*) 120, 121, 122
'Challenging Racism' project 124, 128n7
'Channel' programme 106–107
citizenship 4, 49, 53, 56, 80, 88; and whiteness of French cultural boundaries 63, 65, 68, 69
civil rights 96, 105, 121
Clarke, Peter 101, 104
classism 15
Clinton, Hillary 20, **20**, **21**, 21
Collectif Contre l'Islamophobie en France (CCIF) 120, 121, 122
collective worship 104
colonialism 3, 51, 52
colonisation 64, 68, 69, 124
colour racism 30, 42, 43
colour-blindness 46, 51, 53, 54, 57, 58, 63, 65–66
Combahee River Statement 128n7
common history 29

'condition blanche: Réflexion sur une majorité française' 47
Copblock app 120, 128n3
Copwatch app 120, 127, 128n3
Crenshaw, Kimberlé 30, 97
Critical Race Theory (CRT) 2, 8; and securitization of Muslims in education 95–110
Critical White/Whiteness Studies 2, 83
CRT (Critical Race Theory) 2, 8; and securitization of Muslims in education 95–110
Cullors, Patrisse 116
cultural boundaries, in France 63–75
cultural identity 51, 58
cultural markers 56–57, 100, 109
cultural norms, in France 69–75
cultural policy, in France 5, 63, 64, 65, 69, 70, 71, 72, 73, 74, 75
cultural racism, in France 69
culture: as defined by the institution 70–71; as defined in relation to immigration 71–74

'Danishness' 35
De Gaulle, Charles 55, 70
decolonisation 69, 72
democracy 14, 15, 19, 71, 80, 81, 99–100; and fractal logics of nation in danger 29, 35, 39
Democrat Party 20, 21
democratic values 29
demos 7, 10, 12, 15, 18, 22–23
denial, of race and racism 51, 52, 79, 81, 82, 83, 116, 125
Denmark: Danish People's Party 35; as nation in danger 29–43; public swimming pools 37–40; values 30, 32, 35, 39; white nationalism 30–31
descent 29, 37, 68
difference, racial *see* racial difference
digital technology *see* smartphone apps
discrimination 3–4, 8, 41, 49, 79, 81, 95, 98
'disembodied presence' 125, 126
'disembodied whiteness' 126
disenfranchisement 12, 14, 16, 18
diversity 7–8, 51, 55, 58, 69, 70, 89–90, 104; and whiteness, populism and racialisation of UK and US working class 11, 12, 14, 15, 17, 18, 22
Du Bois, W. E. B. 4–5

economic migration 72
education, securitization of Muslims in 95–110

elite anti-racism 15
elite driven racism 22
'embodied absence' 125–126
embodiment, racialised 114–128, *123*
entitlement 6, 14, 30, 80, 92
epidermalization 126
ethics 2, 116
ethnic categorization 7, 46, 47, 51, 53, 57, 65
'ethnically ambiguous' minorities 5
ethnicity 47, 51, 52, 55, 56, 59n7, 59n9, 63, 69; and fractal logics of nation in danger 29, 30, 31, 34, 40, 41, 42
ethnography 6, 7, 31, 46, 47, 49, 84
eugenics 3
Europeanness 48, 51, 58
Everyday Racism (app) 118, 122, 123, *123*, 125, 126, 127
everyday racism (term) 96, 114, 122, 123, 125–126, 127, 128n7
exclusion 4, 29, 34, 37, 43, 48, 51, 52, 55, 57, 65–66, 116, 121
extremism 99, 100, 102, 103, 106, 109; violent 101, 106, 108, 109

Fanon, Frantz 52, 58, 125, 126
far right 6, 7, 46, 50, 51, 58, 66, 121–122; and whiteness, populism and racialisation of UK and US working class 10, 12, 13, 14, 15, 21, 22
Farage, Nigel 11–12, 13, 16, 18
FBV (Fundamental British Values) 96, 98–108
'Foreigner Policy' 32–33
'foreignness' 37, 43
fractal logics, of a nation in danger 2, 29–43
fractal scalarity 31, 37, 39, 42
Français de souche (far right group) 121–122, 128n5
français de souche (term) 54–55
France 7, 17, 30; citizenship 56–57, 68; cultural norms 69–75; cultural policy 5, 63, 64, 65, 69, 70, 71, 72, 73, 74, 75; cultural racism 69; identity 46, 48, 50, 57–58, 73; Republicanism 49, 52, 53, 55, 58; secularism 74; whiteness 46–59, 63–75
free speech 15
French Melting Pot 67
Frenchness 52, 55, 63, 67–68
Front National 51, 58
Fundamental British Values (FBV) 96, 98–108

INDEX

gamification 114, 122
Garza, Alicia 116
gaze, the 38, 116, 127
gender 14, 17, 18, 38, 39, 84, 98
geopolitics 3
Germany 35, 51, 58, 72
Goldberg, David Theo 50–51, 57, 59n7, 97, 115
Gove, Michael 100, 101
Greeks, in America 17

hate crime 22
Hidalgo, Anne 47, 121, 122
historical privilege 5
Hook, Derek 118, 125, 126

identity: cultural 51, 58; French 46, 48, 50, 57–58, 73
ideology 5, 32, 57, 103, 117; French Republican 7, 47, 49, 54
Ignatieff, Michael 33–34
Illuminations 1
immigration 34, 48, 51, 57, 58, 81, 88, 103; and whiteness of French cultural boundaries 63, 64, 67–68, 71–74, 75; and whiteness, populism and racialisation of UK and US working class 13, 14, 15, 16, 17, 18, 21, 23n2
inclusion 4, 49, 52
inequality 6, 15–16, 17, 22, 34, 35, 75, 118
integration 5, 7, 30, 38; and whiteness of French cultural boundaries 64, 66, 67–68, 72–73, 74, 75n2
interest convergence 8, 105–108
International League against Racism and Anti-Semitism, The 47, 121–122
intersectionality 16, 30
invisible whiteness 83
Irish Catholics 16, 17
Islam 13, 37, 42, 100, 109
'Islamic radicalism' 100, 101, 109
Islamist terrorism 30, 101, 106
Islamophobia 13, 18, 30, 35, 50–51, 120–121
Islamophobia Watch app 120, 121, 127

Jacobson, Matthew Frye 16–17, 67
Jews 16, 17, 83
Jim Crow 16, 42–43, 68
Jyllands-Posten 40, 41

Kaufmann, Eric 14, 51
Khan, Sadiq 95
Kidd, Benjamin 3

labour migration 16
laïcité 63, 74
Leave vote *19*
Leave.EU 13
Lévi-Strauss, Claude 69, 73
LICRA (*La Ligue internationale contre le racisme et l'antisémitisme*) 47, 121–122
look, the 116, 117
lynching 116

McCain, John 20, **20**, **21**
Maghrébin-origin immigrants in France 47, 48, 49, 53, 54, 55, 56–57
Malraux, André 70, 72
Mandelbrot, Benoît 36
'methodological whiteness' 14
methodology 48, 49–50, 114, 119, 122–123
middle-class 14, 47, 48, 49, 51, 55, 56, 57, 89
migration 16, 52, 63, 65, 72, 73, 81
Ministry of Culture 64, 70, 71, 72, 73, 74, 75
Mirzoeff, Nicholas 114–115, 116–117, 117–118, 120, 126, 127
miscegenation 68
multiculturalism 12, 30, 66, 67, 81
Muslims: radicalism of 105–106; securitisation of 95–110

nation in danger, Denmark as 7, 29–43
national categorization 41
National College for Teaching and Leadership (NCTL) 104–105
national culture 7, 18, 32
national integration 7
nationality 29, 34, 49, 64, 68, 84, 87–88
nationhood strategies of British-born South Africans 79–92
NCTL (National College for Teaching and Leadership) 104–105
neo-fascism 1
neo-nationalism 30, 31, 32, 33–36, 37, 42
neo-racism 30, 31
Netherlands 51
news media 7, 29, 31, 32, 35
Noiriel, Gérard 52, 67
nonappearance 114–118, 120, 121, 122, 124, 126, 127
non-whiteness 5
normalisation 2, 7, 10, 21, 22, 85–86, 96, 97
normative whiteness 83
North African immigrants in France 47, 48, 49, 53, 54, 55, 56–57
Nyanspo festival 46–47

Obama, Barack 20, **20**, **21**, 21, 57
OFSTED (Office for Standards in Education, Children's Services and Skills) 101–103, 104, 109
Othering 30, 35, 41

'paranoid nationalism' 33
Park View Educational Trust (PVET) and school 102–103, 104, 109
Pearson, Charles 3
people, the 7, 10, 12, 15, 18, 22–23
petits blancs 66–67
pluralism 79
political elites 32
'poor Whites' 66–67
populism 1, 2, 10–23, *19*, **20**, **21**, 29, 66, 83
populist racialization 10, 11
post-Apartheid South Africa 6, 7, 79, 80–81, 83, 86, 90–91
'post-race' state 12, 79, 80
post-Segregation society 6, 66
power 3–4, 6, 34, 82, 91, 96, 116, 117; relations of 51, 53, 84; white 80, 84, 98; and whiteness, populism and racialisation of UK and US working class 11, 12, 16, 17, 22
pre-criminality 106
Prevent counter-terrorism strategy 99, 100, 101, 106, 108, 109
Prevent Duty 105–106
Principles of Western Civilisation 3
privilege: racial 1, 5; white 2, 5, 7–8, 16, 34, 35, 86, 92
public swimming pools 37–40
PVET (Park View Educational Trust) 102–103

Race, Class and the Racialised Outsider 16
racelessness 97, 123, 125, 126
racial categorization 50, 57
racial characterization 50
racial construction 65–66, 68
racial difference 7, 8, 57; and whiteness of French cultural boundaries 64, 65, 66, 67, 68, 69–70, 75
racial Europeanization 50
racial formation 46, 47, 48, 52, 57, 59n7
racial hierarchy 2, 3, 53, 65, 117
racial inequality 6, 34, 98–99, 118
racial justice 97
racial mixing 68
racial privilege 1, 5
racial reasoning 29, 31, 43

racial segregation 6, 42, 68, 80, 81, 82, 83, 84–91
racial self-interest 1, 14–15
'Racial self-interest' is not racism 14
racialization 35, 42, 69, 73, 89, 108; and CRT 97; culture as basis for 69; and fractal logic 29, 31; of Frenchness 57–58, 68; of Muslims 95; of nationalism 4; of non-white minorities 5, 7, 8, 47, 54; populist 10, 11; of working class 7, 10–23, *19*, **20**, **21**
racialised classism 15
racialised embodiment 114–128, *123*
racialised inaction 114
racism: anti- see anti-racism; anti-Muslim 30; colour 30, 42, 43; cultural 69; elite anti- 15; elite driven 22; everyday 96, 114, 122, 123, 125–126, 127, 128n7; neo- 30, 31; reverse 15; social desensitization to 96–97
radicalisation 21, 74, 106, 107, 110
RE (Religious Education) 104
refugees 12, 13, 17, 29–30, 32, 33
religion 38–39, 63
religiosity 105–106
Religious Education (RE) 104
religious influence 104
religious intolerance 100
religious radicalism 7
Republican France, understanding whiteness in 46–59
Republican ideology 7, 47, 49, 54
Republicanism, French 49, 52, 53, 55, 58
reverse racism 15
right-wing politics 6, 14, 22, 34, 83
Rockwood Academy see Park View School
Romney, Mitt 20, **20**, **21**, 21
Runnymede Trust 17, 18

SACREs (Standard Advisory Councils for Religious Education) 104
Sarkozy, Nicolas 55, 57, 63
school inspection see OFSTED
school segregation 40–42, 42–43
secularism 7, 74
securitization 33; of Muslims in education 95–110
security 13, 30, 86; and Muslims in education 95–96, 97, 98, 100, 105, 108, 109
segregation: of ethnicities 40–42; racial 6, 42, 68, 80, 81, 82, 83, 84–91; of schools 40–42, 42–43; of swim classes 29, 31, 37–40, 42–43

slavery 16, 17, 52, 59n7, 65, 97, 116
'slippery slope' strategy, the 39, 40
smartphone apps 114–127, *123*, 128n3
SMSC (Spiritual, Moral, Social and Cultural' development) 99, 100
social class 19, *19*, 98
social constructionism 42, 47–48, 51, 69
social Darwinism 3
social desensitization, to racism 96–97
Social Evolution 3
social media 31, 37, 38, 39, 41, 115, 127
social reimagination, of racial segregation 85, 89–91
social relations 4, 79, 80, 91, 97, 108
social structures 84, 92
social supremacy 82
'sousveillance' 118, 120
South Africans, whiteness and nationhood strategies of British-born 79–92
Southern Italians, in America 17
'space of appearance' 116–117, 117–118, 123
'Spiritual, Moral, Social and Cultural' development (SMSC) 99, 100
Standard Advisory Councils for Religious Education (SACREs) 104
state-sanctioning 7, 116
Stop and Frisk app 120, 128n3
swim-class segregation 29, 31, 37–40, 42–43
Swiss national and cultural identity 51

temporal reimagination, of racial segregation 85–87
terrorism 21, 96, 99, 101, 106, 107, 108
Tometi, Opal 116
'Trojan Horse letter' 96, 101–105, 109
Trump, Donald 7, 10, 11, 12, 13, 14, 15, 16, 18–19; and presidential election 19, *19*, **20, 21**, 22

UK Independence Party (UKIP) 13, 14
United Kingdom: Brexit *see* Brexit (British Exit); Muslims 95, 99, 105, 107, 108, 109–110; values 96, 98–108

United States, whiteness, populism and racialisation of working class in 7, 10–23, *19*, **20, 21**
universalism 121

values 15, 29, 51, 54, 63, 74; British 96, 98–108; Danish 30, 32, 33, 35, 37, 38, 39, 42, 43
violence 85, 106, 115, 116, 120
violent extremism 101, 106, 108, 109
Virdee, Satnam 4, 10, 12, 16

'Welcome to Country' app 119, 128n2
#WeSeeYou 114, 115
white agency 114
white backlash 23n1, 66–67
white boundary making 5, 63
white bystanders 114, 124
White Condition: Reflections on a French Majority 47
white denial 51, 52, 79, 81, 82, 83, 116, 125
white dominance 3, 6, 80
white identity 10, 11, 14, 58
'White Identity Politics' 1, 14–15
white majoritarianism 2
white nationalism 29, 30–31, 33, 43
white poor 66–67
white power 80, 84, 98
white privilege 7–8, 16, 34, 35, 86, 92
white supremacy 1–8, 53, 57, 58, 80, 108; and anti-racism apps, appearance and racialized embodiment 114, 115–116, 117–118, 122, 126, 127
white talk 86, 87
white working-class revolts 10, 11–15, 18, 20, 21–22
Whiteness of a different color 67
whiteness studies 2, 34, 52, 108
working class 3, 4, 5–6, 7, 88, 89, 98; racialisation of 7, 10–23, *19*, **20, 21**
working class revolts 10, 11–15, 18–19, 20, 21–22

xenophobia 10, 11, 12, 13, 15, 18, 35, 50–51, 58

'zones of appearance' 114, 120

Lightning Source UK Ltd.
Milton Keynes UK
UKHW022338070422
401269UK00004B/37